MULTNOMAH COUNTY LIBRARY, PORTLAND, OR

06

5^{00}

GSM

917.883
M613n

NB
7-93

Date due is no longer stamped in library materials.

PURCHASED FROM
MULTNOMAH COUNTY LIBRARY
TITLE WAVE BOOKSTORE

MULTNOMAH COUNTY
LIBRARY

9/99

NOTES FROM THE SAN JUANS

BOOKS BY
STEVEN J. MEYERS

On Seeing Nature
Lime Creek Odyssey
Streamside Reflections
The Nature of Fly Fishing
Notes from the San Juans

NOTES

from the

SAN JUANS

Thoughts About Fly Fishing and Home

Steven J. Meyers

LYONS & BURFORD, PUBLISHERS

For Debbie

© 1992 by Steven J. Meyers

All Rights Reserved. No part of this book may be reproduced in any manner without the express written consent of the publisher, except in the case of brief excerpts in critical reviews and articles. All inquiries should be addressed to Lyons & Burford, Publishers, 31 West 21 Street, New York, New York 10010.

Printed in the United States of America

10 9 8 7 6 5 4 3 2 1

Library of Congress Cataloging-in-Publication Data

Meyers, Steven J.
    Notes from the San Juans / Steven J. Meyers.
       p.   cm
    ISBN 1-55821-186-1
    1. San Juan Mountains (Colo. and N.M.)—Description and
travel. 2. Fishing—San Juan Mountains (Colo. and
N.M.) 3. Meyers, Steven J.—Homes and haunts—San Juan
Mountains (Colo. and N.M.)
    I. Title.
    F782.S18M48   1992
    917.88'30433—dc20   92-20873
                                    CIP

CONTENTS

PROLOGUE

A few books are all I have. In her sadness my mother threw everything else away, even his photo albums. The pictures taken in the Pacific Theater during World War II, his photographs of airplanes, of tropical islands with exotic vegetation, of army buddies, of himself with short, native women who barely came up to the chest of the five-foot-six-inch man, all gone. Pictures of dark women with brilliant white teeth and shining black eyes, long wavy black hair that framed smiling faces, and ample breasts that rested on round stomachs were thrown away with the albums. Once there were photographs of women wearing grass skirts, their knobby-kneed legs protruding—skinny legs, legs that belied the ampleness above the skirts, legs that bore testimony to the privations of war. Had those same legs run from Japanese soldiers, had they carried those voluptuous bodies only toward my father for a photograph, for an embrace? Had those legs run from everyone, even American GIs? Had they run from everyone but my father?

Is that what my mother was wondering when she attempted to bury her memories?

My own memories of him are sketchy. Images linger, though the photographs are gone, but they are disjointed—fragments, incoherent fragments that rise momentarily without meaning only to sink back into the darkness of deep forgetting. It is from these fragments that I try to piece together an idea of who he was.

There were always women around him. They couldn't resist his eyes, his stories, his lies. My cousins loved him, too, for his stories—especially the one about the golden mountain lion that appeared to him on a hunting trip. It was not a fable, though there was myth in it. I want to believe it was something he had, in fact, seen—a golden mountain lion that could only have been seen with his eyes.

His father had abandoned them, his crippled mother, his sister, him. He had been forced to leave school after the sixth grade to go to work, because there was no one else to support the family. He delivered milk on a dairy wagon, driving a team of horses, hauling milk bottles. What little escape he found as a child he found in the woods. Stories of deer and bear, of brook trout, of the thick, dark woods of a Northeast that no longer exists are the only ones of his childhood he ever told. The stories of his deprivation were told to me by others.

He left home at sixteen to enlist in the army. My mother told me that he lied about his age. Surely, he was older at sixteen than others his age. He had been robbed of his childhood, and the army must have seemed a better alternative to him than staying home.

I never heard a word about my grandfather when I was growing up. He reappeared when I was in high school, but I was never allowed to meet him, not even after we found out that he was dying. My father knew where he was, but he never visited.

The army might have been a good career, if there had been no war. He was airborne, what they called in those days, a Raider. He was sent to the Pacific, and spent the war dropping onto enemy-held islands to secure hostile ground so the troops that followed might land safely from the air and the sea. His body carried ugly scars from wounds that would have removed lesser men from battle and given them a ticket home. His left thigh was atrophied, the knee badly marked and always swollen from a bayonette that had ripped through his leg. His back was bent, and he limped when the weather was damp and cold. There were bullet holes in various parts of his body. I suspect he felt he had no home other than the army so he always went back into battle, patched up, to fight again. Maybe he liked life on the edge. Some of those who knew him well would tell me stories when my mother wasn't around. He was a hero, they'd say. In a few battles he was the only survivor from his platoon. Once he single-handedly held an airstrip against the Japanese for the landing of equipment and troops. For all of this he was decorated with medals, medals to go with his scars, both visible and invisible.

There were articles about him in the home-town newspapers. My mother read them, and was proud. Their story reads a bit too much like a movie from the forties—they met at a USO dance early in the war and fell in love; after the war, they were married.

In the bedroom closet of the room I shared with my brother, there was a jacket. It might have become my most prized possession, but it too was thrown away by a wife who was trying to forget. It was a sergeant's dress jacket with three up, two down on each bicep. On the sleeve, covering the forearm, there were hash marks from re-enlistments. Over the breast there was an airborne insignia—a parachute surrounded by wings. Going up from the pocket, onto the broad shoulder, there were ribbons from battles and campaigns, ribbons from each of the islands he had fought his way across, groping toward Tokyo.

I remember a trip to California I made with an uncle, one of my mother's nine brothers. We ran into an old family friend who remembered my father. "Your father was a hero," he told me. "What eyes he had. What stories." My uncle said nothing. To this day he says nothing. He has never seen a golden mountain lion, and he doesn't believe in them. Although children and women were paralyzed by my father's eyes and smitten by his charm, sensing the unspoken events that lay behind the presence of this strangely powerful man, other men (except those who knew him, who spent time in the woods with him) seemed to fear him.

Twenty-six years ago, on a cold January day, my father took me to Newark's Penn Station to catch the train that would take me back to Chicago and college after a visit home. He smiled and waved to me from beyond the window of the railroad car as it moved away. I smiled too. I loved him, and although I never acknowledged it (from embarrassment or devotion to my brother, I'm not sure which) I knew that I was his favorite child.

When I returned home the furniture was new, all evidence of him was gone, except for his books. I never saw him again.

He left home shortly after my visit from college, shortly after he had placed me on the train and waved goodbye.

I expected to see him when I returned from school. I found out that he was gone when I came home in the spring. The letters I wrote home had been written to both my mother and father. I wrote a great deal about things that would only matter to him— how I was doing on the soccer team, how well I had shot at a rifle competition (he had been my shooting coach through child-hood). My mother wrote back for both of them, which didn't seem strange to me. He had never written, he didn't care much for letter writing, and I never suspected that I had been writing to a chimera.

In my family books are sacred. Although grief drove my mother to dispose of his wonderful collection of shotguns and rifles, to throw the collected photographs of years of war into the trash, to remove his dress jacket from my closet, she could not bring herself to destroy books.

As children we were taught to kiss a book if it dropped to the floor. We hugged books like we hugged each other. We were told that they held the record of thought, of wisdom, of life. Maybe it was an oversight. My father's books were in a set of shelves that was partially covered by the bedroom door.

From those shelves I took three books, when I discovered that he was gone. I would like to have had a few guns, a fishing rod or two, some photographs from the war, his dress jacket— him. In their absence, the books will do. No one knows where he is. Or if he is. The books will have to do.

One is a strange volume of French plays by a playwright who has fallen into obscurity with the passage of time; it is an historical curiosity of social-realist theater, *Three Plays by Brieux*. The book includes "Maternity," "The Three Daughters of M. Dupont," and "Damaged Goods." The fundamental theme of all three plays is feminist, and while they sometimes drag they are quite powerful. What, I wondered, was a man like my father doing with a volume of French feminist theater?

Another book that I found was the 1951 edition of *Troubled Sleep* by Jean-Paul Sartre. The literature of existentialism spoke clearly and powerfully to me. One of the appealing attributes of this non-discipline lay in its amorphous definition, in the fact that men like Sartre and Camus could vehemently argue that they had absolutely nothing in common, yet find themselves strangely lumped together in survey courses—in the philosophy department, in literature departments. To me existentialism's greatest attraction was the fact that one studied it rather poorly in philosophy class, that one began to feel it, to own it, only as literature, only as art. And through it one came to know that art was not an academic notion, but a distillation of the passion, pain, and pleasure of life, real life—life as we are forced to live it. I found one of existentialism's seminal works hiding on my father's shelves at a time when that literature meant a great deal to me. I would have given anything for the opportunity to talk with him about it.

The third book that I quietly liberated from the collection and added to my own set of artifacts was an English edition of Thomas Mann's *Joseph and His Brothers*, published in the year of my birth, 1948. More than anything else I have of my father's, this book connects me with him. It is a retelling of the biblical story of Joseph, with lengthy forays off the main route.

A section on time begins the book. It is something that I carry with me as immediately as my memory of this morning's sunrise. It is as meaningful and real to me as my son's smile. It is literature that articulates human understanding, and human ignorance; the aching of want, and the quiet peace of acceptance. It is, in fact, what anything worth reading ought to be: true.

> Very deep is the well of the past. Should we not call it bottomless?
>
> Bottomless indeed . . . For the deeper we sound, the further down into the lower world of the past we probe and press, the more do we find that the earliest foundations of humanity, its history and culture, reveal themselves unfathomable.

All of this must seem rather ordinary to those with a few literature courses behind them. I hope not, but suspect it is the case. We roll names off our tongues like so much spit. Camus.

Sartre. Mann.

But such was not the reading, the owning of books to my father. He had to leave school as a child. He worked to support a family. He was asked to be a man before it was time, because his father had deserted them, because his mother was a cripple. He joined the army to escape his misery, and found war. He came home unable to leave behind the intensity of experience that is war. He was often feared by others who valued stability because his life of extremes had made him doubt its existence, and he had lost any reason to desire it. He had no friends who could drop literary names. He knew no one who valued anyone who could. He owned these books for the simple reason that he read them. He owned them, and hid them behind the bedroom door. He could not help wanting them, because they were true, and because he was a man whose life had made him one who could tell the difference between truth and a lie.

In the years that have passed since I first discovered my father's absence, and subsequently his presence in these books, I have added other of his volumes to my library. Some are literary, others are outdoor and nature books. None of them mean as much to me as these three. I read them. I hold them and stare at his name inscribed on their opening pages.

I think of my father as an outdoorsman who went to the woods to find peace and meaning. I think of these books as part of the intellectual bequest he might have made me, had he taken the time to make one—the legacy of an uneducated man who might have done much that would have been valued by others had circumstance not stolen his opportunity.

Much of my search for home is tangled up in these fragments. Much of my hunger for home is tied to my search for my father. And I find as I tramp the woods, scramble the peaks, and ply the streams for trout, that his presence is with me, and that all of this reveals itself to me unfathomable.

COMING HOME

The first time I saw them I wasn't prepared for them. Although I had been in the mountains of Colorado before, even backpacked through the Sangre de Christo Range on a vacation trip a few years earlier, the San Juan Mountains took me by surprise. I had driven from Chicago to Utah to photograph in the desert for a few days. Before seeing the San Juans I had traveled through the plains, into other mountains to the north, and through the desert and canyon country of Utah.

The plains have a quiet beauty that captured my interest slowly. At first it was just so much open space, beautiful open space perhaps, intriguingly different from the landscape I had grown up with in the East, but it took a while for the plains to grow from a curiosity to a place of visual delight. A few road trips through the Midwest made them more familiar, and a little time there revealed their great beauty. There are stretches of land that sit pool-table flat beneath the sky, but there are gentle hills, too, where the land rolls off into the distance, undulating. Color and light dominate because the terrain is gentle. Texture is apparent—the soft fuzz of wheat fields seen from a distance, the rougher fabric of a field that is sown in corn. Plowed dirt bakes beneath the sun, neat rows of overturned earth cover the landscape, plowed brown against unplowed amber. It is a landscape that is more subtle than overwhelming, although the sky and the scale are overwhelming enough.

Everywhere in the plains there is evidence of man. The plains embody all of the complex meaning of the word "picturesque"—the boundary between man and nature, the appearance of beauty in the ordering of natural elements. Neat farms sit in the middle of plowed and growing fields. Center-pivot irrigation yields an odd vista of perfect circles of green. Roads lie arrow-straight along section lines, as if drawn on the earth with a giant ruler.

I drove through the plains with alert eager eyes, but by the time I reached the foothills of the Rockies my eyes and body were weary. A short night in Denver did little to relieve the road weariness, and the next day of driving through the mountains was not one of wonder, it was one of survival. I was eager to get to the desert, to begin photographing. The miles passed along the Interstate until I left the broad highway for narrow, two-lane blacktop. The pavement ended shortly past the Colorado-Utah border. Snaking through the canyon of the Colorado River, crossing the river on an ancient wood and cable suspension bridge outside Cisco, Utah, the road brought me to the canyon and slickrock country near Moab. There, I worked—sleeping on the ground beside the car, rising early to catch the morning light, eating breakfast only after the sun rose too high for good light, crawling into my sleeping bag shortly after dark, only to rise again before dawn.

Here the large trees of the mountain forest had disappeared, and in their place ground-hugging grasses, rabbitbrush, and sage grew as widely separated bunches. The piñon and juniper that stood above the scrub were twisted and tortured by this dry place. The character of the desert was quite different from that of the land through which I had been driving. This was not the plains, and it was not the mountains. Brief visits to Moab revealed something else: the people were different, too.

Moab has become fashionable in the past few years. Mountain bikes have become the preferred method of backcountry transportation. Hordes of cyclists roll around the slickrock and into town on fat, knobby tires looking for burgers and fries. The river rats are there, having staked out the town long before the bikers, knowing that access to the big water of the western rivers is nearby. In the West, river runners are desert lovers too. Moab, sitting in the middle of some of the most spectacular desert canyon country, canyons through which the Green and Colorado rivers flow, is a natural place for a desert or river rat to settle. But before these relative newcomers, the fat-tire bicyclists and river runners, there were others.

Once the center of a uranium mining boom, Moab attracted adventurous prospectors. Unlike the mountain men who roamed the hills looking for gold, hunting elk and deer for meat, camping in the shadow of snow-capped peaks while their horses drank from clear streams (and about whom we have woven countless romantic tales) there seems to be far less romance or national mythology based on the life of the desert prospector. What little evidence I have seen of such romance comes from Twenty Mule Team Borax boxes, a younger Ronald Reagan, and tales like those of *Death Valley Days*. No coonskin caps, no bearskin coats, the desert people wore broad-brimmed hats and light clothing. Their faces quickly withered to match the deeply furrowed, dry land. The furrows in their brown faces were as deep and brown as the dry arroyos. The rattlesnake was their familiar. Those of us who lived elsewhere knew little about these tough men of the desert, but in and around the desert country there are legends and myths. Today the descendents of the prospectors and miners who settled here populate the desert towns.

Before the prospectors, and throughout their tenure, there were cattlemen. Running cattle on land that measures a spread's ability to feed cows on the basis of acres per unit (and not the other way around) is a tough job. The results of a life spent ranching in the canyon country can be seen on a face too.

I saw those faces in the Westerner Grill, at the Co-op food store, and the Husky gas station. I heard the wrinkled faces speak. Slow, clear speech. Slow like long summer days in the sun. Clear like the dry desert air. The people reflect the place, and this I would discover as I continued to travel, is the way it is everywhere people settle and make a life, everywhere people stay for a few generations, everywhere people put down roots in the land. I hope it never changes. I hope we never begin to look and speak like the homogeneous, characterless anchorpersons on network news.

Although the desert was a place in which I liked to work; although I found myself in awe of the slickrock landscape, the deep canyons, the violent rivers, the ghostly forms of mushroom rock, natural bridges and stone arches; although the landscape lent itself to photographic abstraction (being, in a sense, pre-abstracted by the effects of rainless months and harsh, dry, eroding winds); it was not a place I could ever call home. But leaving the desert and driving back to Chicago through the southern Rockies I discovered a place that would become home for me. I went there blind. I drove through it in wonder. The experience changed my life, forever.

The route was chosen largely in ignorance. Not knowing the mountains, and having too many of an eastern city person's pre-conceptions about the West, I expected the mountains of southwestern Colorado to be very much like those of central Colorado. Still, I thought it might be a good idea to take a different route. The map showed an orange dotted line along the highway between Durango and Ouray through the San Juan Mountains, a *Scenic Route*. Why not?

Driving out of the desert on U.S. Highway 666, The Devil's Highway, between Monticello, Utah, and Dove Creek, Colorado, the desert mountains retreat in the rear view mirror. The Abajos and LaSalles, mountain massifs that stand alone, surrounded by plateau and canyon, became ever more distant; before me the great mass of the San Juans began to assume prominence. On the cut-off between Dolores and Mancos, Colorado, many of the great features of the Four Corners regions are simultaneously visible. Behind, the desert mountains fade. To the south, the Sleeping Ute slumbers, and Shiprock looms above the southern desert. Mesa Verde parallels the path, deeper into Colorado. And to the north the great immensity of a massive and confused jumble of high mountains asserts itself, dominating even this grand landscape.

Durango sits in the foothills of the San Juans, on the edge of a separated mountain group, the LaPlata Mountains. The south end of town looks a bit like canyon country. Above the Animas River lavender sandstone cliffs rise. The brush is that of the high desert—rabbitbrush and sage. The Mesa tops are green with hay, and what few trees exist are mostly piñon and juniper. The north end of town is all foothills—scrub oak, and pine. High ridges confine the town to the valley of the Animas, and the highway climbs this valley northward into the high San Juans.

The pine and oak gradually give way to fir and aspen, Coal Bank Hill (a climb that would be a major pass anywhere else) tops out near 11,000 feet some thirty miles north of Durango. In that short distance the road has traveled from the edge of the desert into a near alpine world. The tundra and the rocky peaks are visible nearby. I drove this road and ascended into another world. These mountains were not the same as those I had seen before.

Around the corner at the top of Coal Bank Hill, just above the plunging twists and turns of a road that falls into the Lime Creek drainage, Twilight Peak came abruptly into view, its steep flanks falling away deep below me into the chasm that holds the creek. I pulled off the road and stared, mute, into a forest as dense as any I had ever seen. Dark and mysterious it lay before me, spruce and alpine fir covering the steep slopes below; high, sheer mountain faces loomed above. It was a glacial valley as lovely as any I had ever imagined, a range of mountains as grand as I believed mountains would be when as a child I dreamed I might someday see them. Above all of this was a sky so deep, so clear I could never have imagined it. Stunned, I pulled back onto the road and drove on, cresting Molas Pass a few miles later still mute, still dumb with awe. Again I stopped, this time above Molas Lake, and I sat to watch as the sun moved low in the west, illuminating the receding ranks of the Grenadier Range with red-orange light. Near perfect pyramids, these mountains rise in the midst of the jumbled, volcanic San Juans, an anomaly of steep, smooth quartzite, a group of peaks all nearly 14,000 feet high running in a straight line to the east along Elk Creek toward the Continental Divide. I sat there not quite knowing what it was I was feeling, but firmly believing that I would someday return. That feeling was one of primal discovery. I had found, without even knowing that I had been looking, my home.

There are a few things I know as certainly as one can know anything, and so many more things that I do not know. I know that in the depths of the soul, the part of us that screams for understanding, there is little real understanding. I know that there is a difference between kindness and cruelty. I know there is good and there is evil. And that there is love. I know there is an idea we name home, but I know only a little of what this idea means. I know the place of our birth affects our understanding of the world. I know that in spite of this only a part of our understanding is cultural. Some of our understanding is genetic, and some of it derives from the shape of the earth, the form it takes around us.

A favorite biologist, Edward O. Wilson, argued that our vision of the ideal home is the genetic residue of the place that provided safety for us in our distant past as dwellers on the African savanna. So too, I believe, we carry other genetic residue, some of it less species wide than this primitive vestige. This may explain some of our differences in temperament. Much of this is unfathomable in the particular, but we can gain a sense of its content through metaphor.

It is through metaphor that we understand the unfathomable, and it is in the creation of metaphor that personal mythology exists. I do not know, for example, why trout fishing has become so terribly important to me, but I suspect it is because the trout is an emblem of the place I have found to be home. To a very large extent it is through this emblem that I understand my own urges.

A while back I had to fly to Denver to do some work for the state arts council. The airplane that makes the run is a small propeller craft in which I have flown many times. I've had to hang on to my seat as the airplane pitched and rolled in the turbulence of mountain thunder storms. I usually take along a book to distract me, and to keep my mind off of the fact that my stomach is floating somewhere between my head and my feet. The story I chose to read on that flight was an old favorite, *The Spawning Run* by William Humphrey. I began to read shortly before takeoff, and after a few minutes I was completely drawn in by the tale even though I had read it many times before.

Some time after takeoff I glanced from the book, out the window, and saw the summits of the Needles Mountains in the southwestern San Juans. Flying very close to the mountains in the small airplane, Pigeon and Turret Peaks loomed high and craggy directly before me. Their rocky red summits broke free of the thick snow and ice that filled the valleys and coated the more gentle slopes. Ahead, the jagged pinnacles of the Grenadier Range, peaks I had first seen so many years ago, marched in line, coming closer as we flew north. As they passed beneath me, the mass of peaks gave way to the relatively gentle terrain of the High Divide between Elk Creek and Cunningham Gulch. At the intersection of these two very different types of terrain—north of the crags, south of the gentle, rolling tundra of the Divide, perched on the high boundary where Elk Creek of the Pacific drainage meets Kite Lake and the headwaters of the Rio Grande—directly beneath my window, covered with snow and so close I could almost touch it, was Annabelle Lake. Annabelle was surrounded by a tempestuous sea of rock, ice, and snow that rolled into the distance as far as the eye could see. Sitting as she did, in the middle of a range of mountains that had become my home, Annabelle couldn't help but trigger memories. Framed as she was not only in memory, but in that moment in the metaphors of a favorite story, her sight caused me to become lost in the events and meaning, of my homecoming.

The details are as numerous as those of any life, but some stand out as rich and vivid in memory as in the instant of their occurrence. My son was conceived in the heart of the San Juans in a hallway, just inside the front door of a home in Silverton. It was summer. My wife and I had been apart for several months. She was in graduate school in Denver. The bedroom was too many steps distant, and the urge was too strong to hold in abeyance. That urge yielded a son who grew in this mountain home, protected by the relatively narrow confines of a rural world. Now he stands at the brink of adulthood, and I know that he contemplates leaving. Soon, I suspect, he will leave the San Juans to explore a world vastly different from that of his childhood. Will he return, someday, or find his home elsewhere?

Wrapped around memories of the birth of my son is the memory of Karen, a woman I had known and loved in high school, a woman who had married a gifted painter and lived a separate life in Virginia, a woman whose time on this earth was so filled with tragedy that it can scarcely be fathomed. Her husband was not just gifted. Sadly, he was also tormented by mental illness. He committed suicide, but before doing so he murdered their children. That woman and I found each other again after this tragedy. Thrown together by circumstances we could scarcely imagine, even though we knew them to be true, we made love in the San Juans, years after my divorce from the mother of my child, in the murky days after the awful deaths of the children, and during the brighter years after the darkness lifted a bit.

The feelings we shared so many years before, the aching urgency of adolescent sexuality that was first expressed as awkward fumbling in the tiny bucket seats of a Volkswagen beetle, the love—that we were too young and stupid to know was as wonderful and real as it gets—came back. It had matured. It had been tempered by desperate sadness. It was colored by things we wanted to forget, things that can never be forgotten. Deliciously and unrepentantly in love, we sought solace in each other's company, in each other's bodies. We loved in hallways, in the middle of San Juan streams, on the tundra that surrounds Annabelle Lake. So many times we made love, there, in the tundra that sat below me around Annabelle Lake. In the presence of that passion, at the height of love, Karen died of leukemia.

Along the banks of Annabelle Lake, camped on a tundra made soggy and green by heavy summer rains, I survived a violent midnight thunder storm with Jim Bell, a man who had lived full and hard, many, many years in the mines and among the peaks of the San Juans. Beside Annabelle Lake we cast flies to high-altitude trout, and sipped margaritas as the sun dropped behind White Dome Peak. I'd hoped to fish with Jim for a lifetime, but the weak lungs of a miner claimed him.

The memories came in a torrent as I stared down from the airplane. My heart ached, and there was a lump in my throat the size of Pigeon Peak. My fellow passengers (three of them) read newspapers. I wanted to scream out to them, "Don't you see what we're passing over!" But I remained silent.

My generation, born in the years that followed World War II, has been named *The Baby Boomers.* As we moved through the demographer's charts (like a mouse in the belly of a snake) we grew from indulged children, into hippies, and finally stockbrokers—without missing a beat. I have heard us called, in turn, pampered (in the fifties), a generation that would attack the institutions of capitalism without regard for the consequences (in the sixties), and one that would embrace them in an unprecedented orgy of wealth (in the seventies and eighties). All of these things have occurred to some, but not to all. We have yet to find a legitimate or lasting label.

I find the common theme of my generation in the idea of place, in the loss of physical roots and our attempt to re-establish them. Having lost the comfort of a true home in the mobile, modern era, having lost our connection to the earth after more than a century as industrialized beings, we are looking for something. We are trying to find the way home.

In my adolescence I watched as many of my friends wandered off in search of "America." Earlier generations left the soil looking for work. They flooded the industrial cities. Americans, like Europeans before them, shifted from a rural to an urban population. My generation began to question the wisdom of this move, and in small groups we moved back to the soil. In a mutant revival of nineteenth-century utopianism, some of us went back to the farm. We grew vegetables and made our own crude furniture. We sought God with our hearts, with our heads, and as often as not with the aid of drugs. Much of this movement back to the earth took place without my participation. I never lived on a commune, or even a farm for that matter, but the alienation of the city seemed all too real to me, and it seemed likely that our legitimate roots did not rest in concrete.

The demise of modern Utopianism was predictable. History repeats itself. Here and there communal farms remain, but for the most part they no longer exist, and those who sought to find their homes in them have either found them elsewhere or not found them at all. But the attempt revealed something very real about us: comfortable for the most part, secure in our ability to eat and find shelter, we were free to search for meaning, and for something else. That something else, that thing we call "fit," or, in the language of philosophy, "authenticity," became for many of us the quest (often unconscious) for an appropriate home.

In the years I have been in the San Juans, and called them home, I have repeatedly asked myself, "How do you know that you have found your appropriate place?"

The image of the trout, struggling to exist in the frigid water of this beautiful but harsh place seems strangely appropriate to me as a metaphor for human existence, for my own existence. The memories triggered in that airplane by the sudden view of a place where I had been so happy with people I had so suddenly lost, the silly coincidence of those memories occurring as I read of an American angler caught up in the sometimes absurd rituals of British salmon fishing, the immediacy of Humphrey's connecting the folly of human life and sexuality with the spawning habits of salmon made me consider human life and behavior in terms of the behavior of fish. It is intriguing to think that there is a similarity in the genetic imprint of a salmon that leads him home to spawn and the genetic memory of a human who is restless until he or she has found a place to call home.

I'm not sure if it's true for most people, but I suspect it's true for some. For those who leave the place of their birth to wander, sniffing the waters for clues about where to light; for those who travel, only stopping to put down roots when it feels proper to do so; for those who finally build homes, and not just houses; for those who love, and conceive children, who raise them to cherish not only life and others, but the place of their being; for those who suffer both the joys and indignities of life secure in the visible confines—the mountains, streams, and sky—of a place that is right; for these it is simple: home is where you go to spawn.

Sometimes it seems to me that deciphering the meaning of this simple yet complex statement is as significant a mission as any that a person might undertake. I don't know why my wife and I waited to have a child until we were in this place, but I believe the fact that we conceived and raised one here is significant. I don't know why I feel that the San Juans are home and that the many other places I have lived were not. I'm not sure I will ever be able to articulate the feeling of belonging in a place, but I will try.

Part of *place* lies in a description of the place itself. Some of it lies in descriptions of the people. A good bit of it rests in the sagas of adventure that fill the nights—the mythology of place. Much of it will remain, despite the earnest attempts of story-tellers, forever hidden in the hearts of those who live here. But there is merit in the attempt to tell the tale of place, no matter how difficult the task or uncertain the outcome, because the attempt to tell the story is also part of what it means to have found a home in the San Juans.

JEWELS, SURPRISES, AND SOME REASONS WHY I FISH

Some behavior is necessary. We eat because if we don't, we perish. But there are a lot of ways to eat—and few would argue that the person who lives on peanut butter sandwiches, beer, and Vienna sausage, dipped from the can with slimy, gel-covered fingers, has the same attitude toward food as one who lovingly prepares sushi to be eaten in ceremony with lacquered chopsticks. I choose to believe that virtually all behavior has meaning. I spend a lot of time fishing And I spend a lot of time (probably too much) wondering why. There are stories that I tell, others that I hold in memory. Sometimes they help me understand.

Our hike down to the stream that day was slow. In the past we'd practically run from the road to the water, skipping down the hill above the rock-strewn flats. In the spring the flats below us had been filled with roaring water. Now it was autumn, and the wide, braided, gravel course was mostly dry. In previous autumns we had gone through these flats laughing, searching for the stream that would always appear beyond the cottonwoods confined to its narrow, autumn channel. It was still there this golden autumn, it just took us a little longer to get there.

Karen never fished, and her reluctance raised questions that still haunt me.

"You hardly ever eat them any more, do you?"

"No."

"So why do you fish?"

"Because I love to be here, standing knee deep in the water. I love to see my fly drifting with the current. I like to watch as it is carried by the water, suspended in space over the reds, whites, grays, and browns of the rocks beneath. I need to hear the roar of the rapids and feel the tug of the current against my legs. And I need to see the tiny trout come up to take my fly, to know that they are here, and that they are well, to hold these tiny jewels in my hands and marvel at their color—the red spots, the neon-blue haloes. I want to feel them wiggle, so full of life, and watch them race away, scrambling for cover when I release them."

"But doesn't it hurt them?"

I've never satisfactorily answered this question. I imagine that it must hurt them, but what is the nature of their pain? It certainly seems to scare the hell out of them. At one time I would rationalize my behavior by arguing that I released most of the fish I caught and that the experience they have with me ought to make them a little harder to catch for those who would kill anything they can get their hands on. With perverse logic I justified their pain by arguing that they'd be better off in the long run for the experience. It's an argument we've all heard from our parents, in one form or another, at one time or another, and the logic although convoluted has merit. We learn through experience, and sometimes that experience is painful, but who appointed me the surrogate parent of a fish?

Karen found a spot beside the stream that was bathed in the light she loved most: the broken, golden light of autumn. The aspen on the hillsides and the cottonwood by the creek had turned. The sunlight was tinted in its passage through the leaves. Almost painfully bright where it fell straight from the sky to the earth, it was softened where it passed through the leaves, but everywhere it was yellow-gold and warm.

I fished slowly and carefully in the glide that ran beside Karen's seat. I knew there would be no long walks through the woods today, and this lovely piece of water would be the only one I would fish. Beyond the glide, pocket water held scrappy rainbows. Above the run of broken water, not a half mile distant, a deep pool held some of the creek's largest resident fish. Cottonwood no longer grew to water's edge; instead, aspen lined the banks, aspen that had grown in the clearing made by an avalanche as it plunged to the canyon floor. Fir and spruce grew around the aspen and climbed upward with the valley until they could no longer withstand the exposure of high slopes. Shrinking, becoming stunted and then gradually disappearing altogether, trees were replaced by scrub, and finally tundra. Today we would not hike upstream to the tundra. Karen would sit and I would fish the glide.

It took me about an hour to fish the hundred or so yards of water that Karen could see from her rock. In that time I took a few small brook trout, each a gem, each a mirror image of the others. These brookies were about six inches in length, richly spotted, brilliantly colored, and scrappy.

When the time came to leave the water, I walked to where

Karen was sitting, and together we slowly made our way back to the car.

That was the last time we were together on a trout stream. Karen died about four weeks later, at home, within hearing distance of the springtime roar of the Animas River, the river our favorite creek fed in its journey to the sea. She couldn't hear it from her bed in the low flows of fall, and she wasn't given another spring.

I remember those little fish so well. I remember the light. I remember Karen's smiles when I caught fish, and her sadness in so many of the moments between. I remember, too, other days astream, other fish, other people. I remember canyon walls bathed in red sunlight at dusk. I remember martens and ouzels, deer and elk. I remember falcons and eagles and so many other creatures with whom I have shared rivers and creeks. I remember sleek cutthroat running like torpedos when sensing the bite of the hook. I remember rainbows leaping above my head as I stood stunned beneath them, chest deep in cold water. I remember fat brown trout swimming in the crystal clear water of spring creeks rising with confidence to tiny mayflies, each drifting with the current, part of an armada of tiny sloops with sails aloft. I remember the subtle colors of iridescent-hued salmon as they swam in exhausted circles at the end of a taut line after powerful runs in a gray, choppy river while others of their kind moved upstream around me, the water thick with their presence. I remember the sudden shock of a steelhead's first run, blistering runs and leaps after hours of fruitless casting in water that had begun to seem empty. I remember friends and loved ones who have stood in the water with me, casting their own hopes at the end of a fly line. And I remember one who never cast a fly, who stood, instead, on the bank and asked me difficult questions.

Each of the rivers and streams, each fish, each of the

friends, each loved one, and everything else that has happened on a trout stream stays with me, filling my memories with images of wonder. Every memory is a jewel. I angle to mine these gems, and I find there are few other ways to mine them as well. And that is one reason why I fish.

Large, dark caddisflies fluttered across the surface of the Animas River, but no fish could be seen rising as I waddled in my waders across the road, then floundered down the steep bank toward the water. The river on this May afternoon was high. The spring runoff was in progress, and water from the melting snows of the mountains in the north had brought the river above its winter level, but it was not roaring either. The Animas can be virtually unfishable from April through July in a year of big snow and steady runoff, but this was not a spring of big water. Chinook winds during April had evaporated a substantial part of an already thin snow pack, stealing water from the river. The weather had alternated between hot sunny days and cold cloudy ones, preventing the melt from building to a crescendo. Instead, a few days of high muddy water would follow warm spells, and moderate, clear flows would appear after cooler weather. The fishing was better than it had any business being on a spate stream this close to the mountains in May.

Since there were no visibly feeding fish, I tied a large Wooly Bugger to my tippet, twisted a few hefty slugs of lead to my tippet knot, and went prospecting in the deep holes. Not long after I began to fish I saw a flash in the vicinity of my fly and set the hook. The flash had, indeed, been a fish, and I could feel it struggling at the end of the line as I brought it to the surface. When it came into view I saw a sight that never fails to sicken me. The ten-inch trout had moved near the fly but not taken it, and the fly was not wedged in its mouth. Instead the hook had caught in its belly when I struck. A foul-hooked fish, thrashing about wildly, often injuring itself in the process, is not a pretty thing to see.

After releasing the hook from the trout's abdomen and setting it free to heal (hopefully), I decided that I would not spend this beautiful day dragging the bottom. There were no trout rising, and the better fish in the river (large browns who usually hold near the bottom during the day) would be beyond my reach, but I had no desire to snag another fish. In my fly box I found an Elk Hair Caddis roughly the same size and color as those that dipped and fluttered along the surface of the water. I would fish the remainder of the day dry and take whatever I could get, certain that a few small fish taken on the surface would give me more pleasure than striking at phantoms in the deep and risking another floundering, foul-hooked fish.

The Animas is a fairly large river as it flows southward from Durango toward the New Mexico border, especially in the spring. Large rivers, however, fish like small creeks if you study them a piece at a time. I worked my way up the west bank, dropping my dry fly in eddies, drifting it in slick water, probing the pockets behind and in front of the many boulders around which the river flows. In an hour of fishing I took two more small rainbows from the river. Fewer, I supposed, than I might have taken had I been fishing nymphs or wet flies, but I was having too much fun probing the pockets to change my fly or method.

About ten minutes into the second hour, I cast my caddis into a large eddy of calm water, roughly fifty feet from where I stood. The water there was deeper than the water I had been fishing and I doubted that any fish would come up from its depths to take a fly from the surface. Some water, however, just screams "Fish me!" to a fisherman, and this was one of those places. The caddis imitation landed in the middle of the eddy, sat for a few seconds, and was about to drag when a large snout broke the surface, a huge mouth opened up, and the fly disappeared. Surprised, but not stupid, I set the hook.

As soon as I felt that fish I knew it was a good one. Its motion was purposeful and unhurried. It moved upstream, trying to find sanctuary in its home beneath the boulder that created the eddy in which it had been holding. I was able to turn it, but then was not terribly sure it was a good thing that I had. Moving into the current, the fish ran downstream and I was unable to slow it. I watched my line race toward the broad riffle at the tail of the pool and thought I would lose the trout for sure if it entered the fast water. Fortunately, the turbulence stopped it. It turned before the riffle and headed upstream once again. Beneath the surface of the water I could now see a large trout with my fly securely fastened in the corner of its mouth. After about five minutes, I was able to bring the fish, a torpedo-shaped brown trout, against the butt of my rod, which I held in the water. A series of small wraps placed on the rod for measuring trout (strategically placed at sixteen, eighteen, and twenty inches) told me that this trout measured an honest eighteen inches. I removed the fly from its mouth, and gently released the brown.

In this river the better browns are usually nocturnal feeders, yet I had taken an eighteen-inch brown trout on a dry fly in the middle of the afternoon on a day when I decided to forget big fish and enjoy the simple pleasure of taking small trout on the surface. An eighteen-inch brown had come to the surface, grabbed my fly, and given me five minutes of fight that seemed like much more on a day when I expected nothing more than a few stocked fish. An eighteen-inch brown trout had suddenly and unexpectedly come into my world and surprised me.

About a week before the incident with the brown trout on the Animas, a friend and I fished a small creek near Ridgeway,

Colorado. The stream, Dallas Creek, runs out of the Sneffels Range of the San Juans between Ridgeway and Telluride. It flows through beautiful ranch and farm country, where cattle are raised in lush green bottomland. One of the most photographed mountain ranges in the West rises in the south and parallels the valley; Mount Sneffels, over fourteen-thousand feet high, dominates the scene. Much of the creek water is diverted into fields for irrigation and while this is what gives the valley its lush appearance and makes it possible to grow crops, it severely reduces the amount of water in the creek. In this year of lower-than-normal snowpack, its flow was frighteningly diminished. On the ranch where we fished the creek, a few miles above its confluence with the Uncompaghre River, it was scarcely three feet wide. In a few places it was only a foot wide.

The first trout we took confirmed our fear that any fish we'd catch would be small. It was a four-inch brown. A small creek running through a beautiful valley has a special charm, and small fish are a part of this charm. The water was low and crystal clear. Raccoon tracks in the wet mud along the banks confirmed that we were not the only fish hunters in the area. These trout, even if small, would be fun to catch because they would be wild and wary. Our average cast was barely longer than a seven-foot leader. We spent more time on our knees than our feet. It was creek fishing, not river fishing, and it placed us in more intimate contact with the water than we ordinarily experience on big rivers where forty, fifty, and sixty-foot casts are often the norm. This was an intimate world; fishing here, an intimate experience.

The second trout we caught was another brown, this one a bit larger—about seven inches. We were fishing dry caddis imitations because a quick look at the bottom of streambed rocks revealed more caddis than anything else, but the variety of life in the stream was astonishing. Any good suggestive fly would have worked. After a few minutes of probing the miniature pockets, we came to a deep pool where a tree had fallen into the stream near an irrigation headgate. Bud placed a few delicate casts into the pool, with no success. Graciously he offered me the water nearest the headgate since I was crouched several feet closer to it than he was. My first cast landed, leader limp in a slow flow. Just as Bud was remarking, "You ought to get a nice drift out of . . ." a large trout rose and confidently took the fly, leaving Bud's sentence incomplete in the shock of the rise. I struck hard, possibly a bit too soon. The fly imbedded itself in the thin skin near the very front of the fish's mandible and held there long enough for one leap out of the water before slipping free. I figured it for a pretty big fish, but really wasn't too sure. Bud, who had a better angle, was flabbergasted.

"Do you believe that?" he asked. "He must have been at least fourteen, maybe sixteen inches. That was a helluva fish!"

We were both stunned. That trout was longer than the stream was wide for much of its course. Content, or so we thought, to take six to ten-inch fish, we were surprised by the sudden appearance of a big fish in a small place. We fished on, taking a few more small trout. Just before dusk Bud rose a trout that appeared as large as the one in the headgate from a pool so small you could have emptied it with a five-gallon bucket in one dip. He fished and I watched, as dusk and then darkness surrounded us. The trout never showed again.

There have been many other wonderful surprises in my fishing life, not all of them big fish—finding a stretch of water near home filled with pure-bred cutthroat (a waterfall and highway fill isolating the strain from introduced species) was one such surprise. The most memorable surprise of my fishing life remains the first steelhead I ever felt at the end of my line. I had been fishing for salmon during a run of pinks in the Campbell River and had grown accustomed to the repetitive nature of the strike, run, and slow circling of these uniformly sized fish when my drifting fly stopped in mid-swing (the pinks had been taking a Babine Special as it hung in the water at the end of a downstream swing). I raised my rod and suspected that I had snagged on a rock in the split second before the hook was set, but that illusion was quickly shattered as my line began to knife through the water toward the heavy current in the middle of the river; then it followed the sea-run monster downstream, back toward the brackish water at the meeting place of the Campbell and Discovery Passage. My drag was set to its maximum and I pressed on the exposed rim of my reel spool until my hand burned, but nothing slowed the fish, the noisy reel, or my pounding heart. When my reel arbor appeared between the fast-disappearing wraps of backing, I grabbed the spool hard with my right hand, trying to save my fly line, and felt an incredible pull as the leader stretched to its limit and finally snapped. My line went limp and the steelhead disappeared in the choppy water.

Anglers are often asked why they fish. Fly fisherman, in particular, are asked why they fish the fly, when seemingly easier, sometimes more effective, means for catching fish are available. The answers that have been written in response to these questions have often been eloquent. Frequently they have been beautifully worded defenses of sport and of the choice of elegance over brute pragmatics. Sometimes they state a preference for the simple pleasures of angling, pleasures derived from close contact with a world where natural processes are obvious and are not obscured by the intervention of complex social and economic institutions. Often analogies are drawn between the limited world of angling and the broad world that includes all natural events—we understand the big picture by seeing a smaller one clearly. I have contributed some of my own thoughts in the past and I will continue to try to explain why I would rather cast a fly than a lure or bait. I will try to make sense out of the fact that given the choice, I'd rather be on a trout stream than in an office. I continue to get lost in the difficult, if entertaining, problem of what it means to be an angler, but I will miss the mark horribly if I say nothing in these ramblings about surprise.

For all the elegance, appropriateness, and metaphor, for all the similarity and dissimilarity between angling and the rest of life, the aspect that makes each day on the stream fresh is the wonderful and sudden shock of surprise. The surprise of a big fish. The surprise of an eagle swooping low. The surprise of a tactic working when it should not, or not working when it should. The surprise of 7X tippets holding and 2X tippets breaking. The sudden surprise of lightning and a thunderclap nearby. The soft surprise of the first scent of moist dirt and pine in a warm spring breeze.

An angler can never learn enough to anticipate everything. If a fisherman ever reaches the point where he can hook an eighteen-incher after landing a handful of small stockers and not be left in shock, if a fisherman could take a sixteen-incher from a small pocket in the trickle that is a small creek and not stand in stunned disbelief, if a person could stare at the quiet water of mid river, line limp after the take, run, and subsequent loss of a sea-run mystery and not feel his heart pounding with the adrenaline rush of sudden surprise, then he ought to hang up his rod and waders forever. Should that day ever come, a fisherman would do better to think seriously about what had become of his wonder than to probe the pockets for trout. Every trout risen ought to be a wonder. Some events experienced when fishing should stun us utterly. There should always be surprise, so far there always has been, and that is another reason why I fish.

The reasons for fishing are many and we talk about them often, but we usually only scratch the surface. There is metaphor in behavior that transcends the immediate experience of an act—metaphor that provides a glimpse into more significant meaning.

I fish because it's fun. Often when I find myself involved in a technical conversation or a discussion of the literature of angling with another fisherman—times when the seriousness of angling seems overwhelming—I step back from the conversation to look at myself. "My, how pompous we have become," I think. "Look at you. You talk about this thing as if it were astrophysics. Try to keep things in perspective, Steve, this is only fishing."

Only fishing. But the simple things we do carry meaning, and while the simple acts of life ought to be filled with joy, that does not mean they are devoid of meaning. It does not mean that simple acts cannot carry profound meaning.

I say this, not because some select, simple acts are terribly important; rather, because all acts contain the possibility. In thoughtful moments, baking bread becomes an overwhelming metaphor for nurturing and sustaining life; the making of a bed a moment for reflecting on the wonder of creation, and the consuming fires of passion. Simple acts—like baking bread, making the bed, even fishing—contain powerful meaning. At times the significance of these simple acts can overwhelm us. We don't choose to think about these things. The thoughts take us because of who and what we are. It would be a mistake to assume because of the content of some angling literature that fishing is more important than other simple acts. It is in the appreciation of the fact that angling is a simple act that its seriousness rests.

The thought of a trip to Montana or British Columbia fills me with excitement; and there are times when I think I'd like to move to a place where the fish run to the sea and come back to the river fat and shiny, where I can watch the tides and smell the salt, but I don't. And as much as I love to fish new water for unknown fish, in the end I am always anxious to come home. It seems I am most happy when fishing the streams of home. I have thought long and hard about the metaphor of my own simple acts, the meaning of my choices, and little that is coherent has emerged, but some things can be glimpsed as I peer into the water, through the reflections of mountains, at the torpedo shadows that dash for cover beneath the dark boulders of a turbulent mountain stream.

My house, when I was a child, was in the middle of a blue-collar town in the industrial Northeast. My house had a white-gray sky above it. To the east, New York City lit the night, and when the haze was thinned by strong winds the skyline was dominated by the tall buildings of midtown Manhattan. The rivers were filled with carp and most of the water had a film of rainbow-colored oil on the surface. My house was in a project of identical buildings, a half-mile row of them, two-story brick, that sat on land that once was a truck farm.

My home had flannel shirts in my father's closet, and Mackinaws of red-and-black checked wool. And fishing rods. The Mackinaws had double-thick shoulders and game pockets in the back. The shirts and Mackinaws smelled of fire, and of evergreen. On the dining-room wall there were rifles and shotguns. In the bedrooms there were the bookshelves. The books that drew my attention when I was a child were not the thick black books with difficult titles, the ones with fine print and no pictures. The books I read in my home were the ones with pictures of grizzly and kodiac, of great cats, of waterfowl. I read nature books in my father's bedroom, as rods waited and guns rested on racks in the dining room, as wool and flannel and the smell of the woods filled the closet.

Stories filled my home in the gray industrial Northeast, but they were not stories of the city. They were stories of the woods, of game, of old friends, and adventure. I listened to them evenings and weekends. And in the morning I watched the teller of those stories board a bus with his tool box, to ride off to fix other men's machines. I watched myself ride off on a bus to sit in an overheated classroom where I would gaze out the window at the dreary sky and wonder, what does a mountain look like? Really? Close up? Will I ever see an elk?

My home stream cuts a watery path through a dense ever-green wood. Elk are thick here and the mountains rise abruptly from the valley I fish without intervening plain. The stream is a gorge between mountains. The sky is deep blue. There are no buses.

Below the water lies mystery. Slippery shadows appear— and disappear. Was it water? A trout? My father? I try to catch them and sometimes succeed. I hold the shadows for as long as I can and then release them, but the mystery remains no matter how many shadows I have held.

I love to fish because it is a simple act. Like baking bread or making the bed.

T HREE-SCORE AND TEN

Call me crazy. What literate angler would admit, in print no less, that he likes to catch fish? Some days I actually try to land as many as I can. Maybe it's projection, but I think there are a lot of otherwise sophisticated anglers out there who feel the same. Just where did we get this notion that fishing has nothing to do with catching fish?

Edward Ringwood Hewitt is highly regarded and justifiably famous. Many consider him to be the father of fisheries management in America. He invented the Bi-visible and the Skater. By virtue of his single-minded devotion to salmonids, his knowledge of what had taken place on the other side of the Atlantic, and his keen observation, he and a handful of others brought American trouting to its initial maturity. I suspect that we will someday forget who gave us the Bi-visible, but we are in no danger of ever forgetting Hewitt's statement about the three ages of a fisherman. It has been nearly seventy years since he wrote the famous words, but they have not faded into oblivion. Quite the contrary, Hewitt's words have been repeated so often that they seem in serious danger of becoming mere cliché. That they have not is powerful testimony to their simple, undeniable truth. Anglers do, indeed, often pass through three stages in their fishing lives: the time when they want to catch all the fish that they can; the time when they strive to catch the largest fish; the time when they study to catch the most difficult fish, caring more for the sport than the fish. I have no problem with his words, or the truth they seem to communicate. It's just that those of us who occasionally want to catch a lot of fish, or maybe a really big one every now and then, stand condemned by Hewitt's discernment and wisdom. It doesn't help, frankly, that every time I pick up a fishing magazine or a new angling book I find Hewitt paraphrased.

A while ago I was fishing on Silver Creek in Idaho with a superb angler I had only just met and whose company I enjoyed very much. A publisher in California was sending me to British Columbia to write about salmon and steelhead. He suggested I stay with his good friend in Hailey on the way to B.C. When I arrived at Silver Creek the famous Trico hatch was on and trout were everywhere. I was told that the Tricos bring every fish in the river to the surface, and this certainly appeared to be true. What I didn't know was that it also brings every angler from Seattle to Bangor to the river as well. Open water was scarce. I noticed something else that was scarce: any variety in the approach to fishing for these beautiful spring creek trout. Every angler worthy of the name had a #24 Trico imitation floating downstream at the end of a 7X tippet. Some were casting to individual trout, others floated the imitation through pods of feeding fish hoping for something to happen. There was no doubt that the accepted technique was dry, #24 spinner imitation, downstream, on a long, thin, slack tippet. End of discussion.

And it worked, sort of. We took many fish this way, but often there was a long wait between takes. During one of those pauses I decided to experiment. I have always been a fan of the late Ken Miyata and his theory of "anting" the hatch. It flies (forgive me) in the face of convention. The theory of established search patterns, especially during profuse long-term hatches, is so much a part of our angling science and technology that only a fool would ignore it. But it has been my experience that educated fish get tired of seeing the same fly for days on end and will take imitations of other insects, sometimes in preference to imitations of the currently dominant bug. I tried an ant with no luck, but once the Trico was off the tippet, the fun of experimenting seized me. I tried a small emerger and finally fished with a variety of soft hackles—not because I thought they looked particularly like Trico spinners, not even because I expected that the fish would take them. There was a possibility, however, that doing something different might help me take a few more fish. My results were no better than they had been with the Trico (they weren't much worse either), but that's not the point. I was having fun.

A few weeks later I spoke with the publisher who had arranged my visit to Idaho and B.C. I asked him what our Idaho buddy had thought about the day we'd spent together on Silver Creek. I was told that the only words he had been able to manage were, "Oh, Steve's a wet-fly man." Wet-fly man? Hadn't we spent an afternoon together taking scrappy rainbows from the Big Wood on Elk Hair Caddis? Hadn't I spent most of my day on Silver Creek floating the Trico Spinner like everyone else? And what if, in fact, I was a wet-fly man? Why did it seem to me that these words were not simply an observation but a judgment? I felt like the miserable son in Kafka's short story who, knowing that he had failed his father in some fundamental and irreversible way (but not knowing exactly how), jumped off a high bridge to his death. I didn't go looking for a high bridge. I guess that's another indication of my moral failure.

My problem with Hewitt having made us aware of what it means to be a mature fisherman is not that he was necessarily wrong in his assessment but that it seems to contradict my conviction that maturity is something we must gain through experience. Too many literate anglers seem to be trying to get there vicariously. Wisdom cannot be achieved by proxy. We cannot short circuit the process simply by reading a good book (although really good books help). And, we may discover (if we are lucky enough to find it at all) that wisdom looks a little different now than it did to Hewitt so many years ago.

I still love to spend a day catching fish, to walk a streambed I know well, probing for trout in the places I have found them before, searching as well in the places they have never been, hoping for a surprise. I have had many a fiftyplus fish afternoon on my home stream, and I have loved every fish, every expectation fulfilled, every pleasant surprise. Often these are easy fish to catch, but I do not wade past them looking for the bigger, more difficult fish. On these days I enjoy them all.

And there are days when I hike along water I know to hold countless easy fish, looking for a spot where I have seen, or suspect, a larger, more difficult fish. I have spent hours working a place I know to hold a lunker. Some days I've gone fishless in the process, but it mattered little.

There are entire trips dedicated to big fish, and weeks and months of fly tying and dreaming inspired by the prospect of a journey to salmon or steelhead water. For those of us who live in the interior, away from the sea-run behemoths of the coastal fisheries, any salmon or steelhead outing is an outing framed in size. What would be the rewards of a maturity that had missed the thrill of a whirling reel, the pounding heart of an angler attached to a Springer? Call me immature, but I rather fancy the prospect.

And then there are the wise choices, choices that indicate that this angler in his forties does, indeed, sometimes show a glimmer of still-distant wisdom. Sometimes I will abandon methods I know to be effective in order to fish in a certain way. Sometimes after pulling trout from a river by drifting weighted nymphs through holding water, I will pause, consider the beauty of a rise to the dry fly, and change my method. Sometimes I will wait for a rise before fishing.

Sometimes a river will teem with feeding trout, dorsal fins, and tails rhythmically porpoising as trout take emerging insects near the surface, while a quiet sipper will dimple the water across a difficult current, methodically taking the eddying dead spinners of a hatch and a fall that has long since passed. What is it but an affirmation of Hewitt's description of the mature angler, to go after that deviant fish, the fish that requires the difficult cast, the fish that will look at a dozen different imitation insects before he finds the one that interests him, the fish that will calmly take control of the struggle once your hook has been driven home and leave you in doubt until the very last instant about the outcome?

The fact is, at my current stage of angling development I contain all of Hewitt's ages of the angler. I suspect most of us do. I cannot know what wisdom will be given to me as I age. I can hope that it will be great, but I can't know that it will be. I certainly will receive no knowledge, angling or otherwise, if I presume to know what that knowledge will be before I have earned it. So I sometimes take a good many fish, I sometimes seek only large ones, and I sometimes go after the most difficult, caring more for the sport than the fish. It's taking me a while to grow up.

THE CANNONBALL CAST AND THE SICK FROG-LURE

A purist can be many things, but there is a common thread in all purist behavior, and that is a rigid adherence to rules. In angling this means the choosing of rules that set limits on technique and tackle. The fly-fishing purist chooses to fish only with an artificial fly; the dry-fly purist, only with dry flies. There are cold-water purists who wouldn't be caught dead fishing for bass, bluegill, or crappie, and I suppose there are other kinds of angling purists as well. I imagine that somewhere there's a purist who chooses to fish only light tippets and small flies, feeling, perhaps, that any fish taken on a leader with a breaking strength greater than one pound has been taken unfairly. The possibilities are endless. I don't mind this exercise of free choice—after all, this is America—but it bothers me when these choices, freely made, are in some way associated with The Eternal Good and imposed on others.

I know some worm fishermen who are wiser in the ways of trout than many in the fly-fishing fraternity, and who fish with a style and grace that any angler might envy. I've known ignorant fly fishermen to chum for trout by shuffling their feet in the streambed, dislodging the worms, eggs, nymphs, larvae, and pupae that reside there, who cast downstream into the invertebrate chowder that they have stirred up; and I have seen them take a lot of fish. This is hardly sporting. Whether one angles with a fly or a worm on the end of the line, a spoon, spinner, plug, or popper, it is not the terminal tackle that determines whether a fisherman is sporting. But this is not to say that I'm without preferences.

Given a choice I would prefer to cast an artificial fly. If there is any hope of taking a fish on a dry fly, I would prefer to take a fish that way. For me, the ultimate angling thrill would be the taking of a large, strong, wild trout, perhaps a fresh steelhead, on a small dry fly; to have the fish take my fly, visibly, on the surface, with confidence, because the fly has been well tied, wisely selected, and properly presented. This is not always possible, however, so I often fish below the surface, and I sometimes search the water for trout where I expect they will be, and not because I have seen them feeding. It is all angling and I love every minute on the stream, whether I am fishing wet or dry. I guess I'm not a purist.

You wouldn't know it to look at me, though. Or to listen, for that matter, either. I have few friends (anglers, and those who have never caught a fish) who have been spared a long monologue on the joys of fly fishing—its history and literature, the evolution of tackle and techniques. I am prone, at the slightest indication of interest (and sometimes even when no interest has been indicated) to launch into conversation (often one-sided) about trout, salmon, and the aquatic insects that they eat. Fortunately, some of my friends actually enjoy these evenings, otherwise I'd have few friends left.

One such friend showed not only tolerance for such conversation but an eagerness to learn and an aptitude for fly casting. Almost from the day I met her, I spoke to her about trout, salmon, and steelhead. I talked to her for hours about imitation, presentation, dead drift, mending, the sudden inch, the Leisenring lift, the induced take; about line tapers and rod actions; about the quiet joy of fishing with a fly. Together, we planned a canoeing and fishing trip up the now-submerged Lake Fork of the Gunnison River, on what is now Blue Mesa Reservoir.

Although Debbie had fished before, she was new to fly casting. Before the trip we spent time together in a nearby park with me coaching and her casting. I was pretty confident that she would be able to take fish with a fly, but I didn't know if she would be able to cast comfortably from a canoe on a windy lake, and I wanted to be sure that she would be able to enjoy the fishing on this trip. As insurance, I threw a few spinning rods into the pile of gear that we were accumulating.

Once we got on the water, we paddled steadily from the put-in to the campsite, trolling spoons behind us (this is something I will often do when canoe camping—the object being to secure dinner, not sport). We arrived in camp early enough to pitch the tent and stow gear, and still leave the last hour or so of daylight for fishing. Grabbing the spinning rods, which were already rigged, we paddled out into the lake to fish with spoons and spinners. The fly fishing would wait until the next day.

Some trout were rising near a long spit of submerged boulders and we paddled toward them. After a few minutes of casting, and no strikes, a tremendous wind came up. Huge waves soon followed, threatening to capsize the boat. Yelling above the wind,

I suggested we head for the calm water of the small cove in which we had situated our camp. Grabbing the paddles, we stroked toward shelter.

As we paddled, I noticed that line was coming off Debbie's reel at a furious pace. Her lure was still in the water and her bail was open. Reaching forward, I closed the bail and we continued to paddle. I'll never know if her lure was taken by a fifty-pound lake trout, if the belly in the line was so long that, dragging through the water, it exerted too strong a pull on the rod, or if the spoon had simply snagged on the bottom, but as we paddled against the wind and the waves, the rod bounced up to the gunnel and hopped over the side. We watched, helplessly, as it slowly disappeared into the opaque depths of the lake.

Finally we reached the shelter of the cove. As we paddled toward shore, I decided to try one last prospector's cast toward a snag that poked above the water about fifty feet out from where a small creek entered the lake. The evening was fast coming to a close, and our fishing for the day would soon end, but there was certainly time for one last cast. There always is. My spinning rod was still rigged with the heavy fluorescent green spoon with Day-Glo orange diamonds that I had trolled with little hope and less luck on our journey into the cove earlier in the day. Don't ask me why I fished it. It seemed to work pretty well on other trips, going through the water at high speed, towed behind the canoe like a keelhauled mutineer. It certainly wasn't a midge. It was not connected to an 8X tippet. You couldn't present it with any delicacy. But it was there, so I cast it.

The cast was about twenty-five feet, and landed by the snag with a kerplunk that was not much different from the sound I'd expect a cannonball to make when shot into the water. I let it sink for a few seconds, then began the retrieve. Immediately a good fish hit, I struck, and a few minutes later a beautiful sixteen-inch brown trout was lying in the boat.

My pride was abruptly deflated by a series of questions from my ardent angling student.

"Steve, tell me what that lure imitates."

"You mean this half-ounce fluorescent green spoon with Day-Glo orange spots?"

"Yes."

"Well, I don't know. Maybe a frog with chicken pox."

"But didn't you tell me that trout fishermen carefully determine what it is the fish are eating and then try to imitate their food?"

"Well, yeah . . ."

"I don't see any sick frogs around, do you?"

"Well, no, but . . ."

"And didn't you spend hours telling me about delicate presentation and drag-free drift and controlling the line and induced movement? What kind of presentation was *that?*"

"Gee, Debbie, this is a spoon; that stuff doesn't apply. Well, it does, but it isn't the same. I mean . . ."

"And, Steve, isn't that a brown trout?"

"Why yes, it is."

"Didn't you tell me that brown trout were sometimes so hard to catch that Fish and Game stocks catchables, because some fisherman complain that the browns aren't?"

"Yeah, but . . ."

"Well, now I'm totally confused. That presentation—what do you call it, the cannonball cast? And that fly, or spoon, whatever, doesn't imitate anything. And the fish you caught is supposed to be the one that's the hardest to catch. What were you doing all those evenings when you made up those long speeches about flies and history and technique—were you putting me on?"

I just looked at her. And she at me. And then we began to laugh hysterically. We laughed so hard we both fell in the water getting out of the boat. We laughed as we pulled the canoe out of the water and trudged up the hill to camp. We laughed whenever we looked at each other during dinner. We laughed through the night.

And the next morning, when I went down to the lake to see about catching a little breakfast, I continued to laugh as I abandoned my fly rod and took the spinning rod and the sick frog lure with me. I damn near fell down, convulsed in laughter when I took an eighteen-inch rainbow and a seventeen-inch brown trout within five minutes of reaching the water. From the water near the snag. With the spinning rod. On the fluorescent green lure with the Day-Glo orange spots.

Natives

"It is not necessary to choose between being a
country man and a city man, as it is to decide, for
instance, some time along in one's thirties,
whether one is an Easterner or a Westerner."
—Edward Hoagland,
Red Wolves and Black Bears

I wasn't born in the San Juan country,
which makes me something of an interloper.
A native is special, and there are places
where the definition is drawn narrow. If you
weren't born here, even if you've lived in the
place for sixty years, you're a newcomer. Hill
people back East, I'm told, feel the same.

About fifteen years ago the local library
got a grant to do some local history. Many of
the folks associated with the library and the
Historical Society were not, strictly speaking,
locals. Some had been in the county all of

49

their adult lives, but not having been born in the area, they were somewhat suspect. Others had moved here as adults. Thinking it would be good to bridge the gap between the newcomers and the natives, the library board planned an Old Timers Night. A list of natives who had seen decades in the San Juans was drawn up, and those on the list were invited to spend an evening telling stories about their lives in the San Juans. The purpose was three-fold: there was a sincere desire to honor our elderly for the richness of their experiences, there was a wish to record our local history for future generations, and there was the hope that such an evening would build a bridge between those for whom the San Juans had always been home and those of us who had come here to find a home after growing up elsewhere.

The honored speakers had all attended school in the San Juans as children. Many had lived through the devastating flu epidemic of 1918 and survived hard winters when no supplies arrived in town for months because of heavy snow and avalanche. All of the panel members had seen the fortunes of the economy rise and fall with those of the mines. Each invited guest could look back at a minimum of fifty years in the place—some as many as eighty. But not all of them, we were to discover, were natives.

About a week before the first program of reminiscence, the library board received a protest letter from one of the proposed panelists. He wondered if the board was aware of the fact that one of the other panelists was not "a local?" A woman who was supposed to speak, a woman who had lived in Silverton for roughly fifty-five years, had not, in fact, been born in Silverton. She had come over Stoney Pass from Creede as a young child, and although she had attended every grade from kindergarten through high school in the Silverton school, although she had married and raised a family here, and despite the fact that she was just now starting to enjoy her husband's retirement from the mine and her grandchildren, she should not (we were told) be considered suitable for the panel.

I found the dispute amazing, not just because an entire life of play and toil, joy and sadness seemed to matter so little in the defining of a local, but because of the irony of the overwhelming similarity between this woman's early childhood and those of the other panelists. Creede, the town where she had been born, is just over Stoney Pass and a few miles down the Rio Grande drainage from Silverton. Creede, too, is a mining town. And Creede also suffers San Juan winters of brutal cold and heavy snow. Creede enjoys a surrounding vista of jagged peaks, just like Silverton. It's not as if the woman had come here from New York or San Francisco!

Rather than cause a ruckus, this kind and considerate woman arranged to be out of town during the evening the panel met. She left behind a wonderfully poetic letter in which she described her childhood memories. The letter was read in her absence and a confrontation over the definition of native was avoided.

All of this has come upon me again, after not thinking about it for many years, because I've been creasing a hat and wondering about native trout.

The native trout in the San Juans (more specifically, on the western slope of the San Juans) is the Colorado River cutthroat. A genetically pure specimen is harder to find than a human native. Just like native people, native trout mix, interbreed, and lose the wonderful color and uniqueness that is theirs before foreign species are introduced. Often they find it difficult to survive. For whatever reason—genetic absorption, failure to compete successfully for available resources, lack of social skill—natives are endangered everywhere, and this is a terrible thing.

In the angling fraternity we use the word "native" with a

degree of vagueness mountain people would find hard to fathom. In the East, the brookie is the native. In the inter-mountain West, the cutthroat is the native. On the Pacific Coast, the use of the word gets complicated by the presence of several native species. But here in the mountains where the term is used to describe all cutthroat, we use it too loosely. The Colorado River cutthroat is at least as different from the Rio Grande cutthroat as the woman who came over the hill from Creede was from the locals in Silverton. More so. At least all of the humans are the same species (at least I think so, though a few times in the San Juan Bar, I wasn't quite sure). These two species of cutthroat are very different from each other. They look different and they don't behave the same. Even cutthroat of the same species are not all the same. We have learned that trout often contain genetic information that is specifically geared toward the demands of survival in a very limited environment. The Colorado River cutthroat of Lime Creek in the San Juans probably doesn't live like the Colorado River cutthroat on Grand Mesa in the Gunnison River drainage. Much of the difference is genetically encoded.

There was a time when you could move slowly across the country and easily hear the changing of speech patterns. Some characteristic sounds were the result of language habits learned in different parts of the Old World, habits that remained intact in the New World. Many of the unique sounds of regional speech are the result of the migration of various ethnic groups. The linguistic map of America is, to a large extent, a map of the movement of immigrants. But this is not the only factor. Some sounds, I am convinced, are the result of a people's living in the shadow of mountains, or upon the broad prairie, in the presence of sweltering heat or biting cold. Hill people sound different from plains people. We are all gradually learning to speak the generic

American English of the Five O'Clock News. It's a shame, but there's no stopping it. Trout, however, don't watch television. With a little intelligence, some control over the introduction of hatchery trout into wild populations, and a desire to preserve trout according to a hill person's definition of native, maybe we can keep the same homogenization from overrunning the trout population.

I mentioned that this rumination about natives (people and trout) came to me as I was creasing a hat. I've got a new Stetson. It was a gift from a good friend back East and came from L. L. Bean. The hat I've been wearing (a big, black Resistol that I bought years back while surveying in the desert outside of Las Cruces, New Mexico) is starting to look frazzled, but the Stetson has seen little time on my head. It needed a change in crease to feel right.

This cowboy-hat business is something of a minor affectation. I am an introduced species myself, a brookie in cutthroat country, and certainly not one who was raised to wear a cowboy hat. I started wearing a cowboy hat when I was working with a survey crew. Each of us wore a black Resistol, Filson vest, western shirt, jeans (held up by a wide belt with a big silver buckle), and pointy toed boots. I'm not sure if the costume was determined by practicality or convention, but it was what we all wore. Except for Kelly, of course, who always wore a white Stetson— but then, I suspect Kelly has always been different. We frequented a bar in Dolores, Colorado—known as the Hollywood— when we came back from the field. The bartender was the girlfriend of one of our crew members and she always screamed, "Here come the bad guys" when we walked in together. That happens some when you wear a black hat. It was a costume, I guess, but it was natural enough.

It's said in the West that a cowboy will settle on a hat brand, model, color, and crease when he's a teenager, and as long as he lives, he'll never change it. Today, as I creased the silver belly Stetson to match my black Resistol, I wondered about the change from the black hat I'd worn for so long, and thought, "Hell, you're not a native anyway, why get all worked up about a hat?" True enough. I suspect I'll fish in the Stetson; and I'll paddle a canoe in it, watching the rain drip away from my face and neck off the wide sheltering brim. I'll be glad on hot sunny days that it keeps the sun off my head, and out of my eyes. I'll be happy when it catches the point of a poorly cast fly, keeping it out of my scalp. I'll break it in until it looks about as ratty as the Resistol. Some day soon it'll probably fit pretty good. The fact that I can change hats says something about me. In part, it says I wasn't born here. But I hope there will always be those who were. People—and trout.

TAILWATERS AND HOMEWATERS

It is ironic that such a conversation would take place where it did, on the Bighorn River in southeastern Montana. A. J. and I were talking about the fishermen who have spent virtually all of their angling lives on the super-fisheries. Below Yellowtail Reservoir, where we were drifting in a wooden McKenzie boat, the controlled releases of water have created a superb trout fishery. From the bow of A. J.'s beautiful boat, I could see trout damn near everywhere. It was spring, and the rainbows were spawning. The browns were on top feeding on Baetis and midges. Pods of brownies sipped from the surface, and gloriously happy trout fisherman were drifting dry flies over them, taking many fish. It was heaven, sort of.

Tailwater fish are often large. On the San Juan River below Navajo Dam, in north-western New Mexico, the average trout is in the neighborhood of eighteen inches. A good angler will rarely have a day without at least one trout in the twenty-inch range taking his fly. In tailwaters the fish are often plentiful. I have seen anglers fish water where trout were so thick that an entire afternoon would be spent casting, hooking, and playing fish, without having to move more than fifty feet between lunch and the final trout of the evening. Tailwater fishing can be extraordinary fishing, but it is not without its problems.

I fish the San Juan River below Navajo Dam a lot. I work there as a guide. I play there, too—fishing on my days off, trying to keep in touch with the hatches as they move up and down the river, spending time with my fishing buddies who are there on their days off as well. I fish there in the winter when other streams are asleep beneath the snow. I would be lying if I were to say that I don't love it, but fishing this tailwater can raise some unique questions. Where else can you become angry when a beautiful seventeen-inch trout takes your fly, because you were aiming at a twenty-inch trout only a few inches away? Where else can you become so used to good fish taking your fly that you find yourself becoming jaded? And what could be worse for a fisherman than to find his passion, his excitement, his wonder being dulled by excess?

Contrast this with the experience of fishing the small, uncontrolled stream, the spate stream that is scoured by runoff, that slows to a trickle in dry years, the stream that is surrounded by dense brush, and populated—sparsely when compared with a tailwater fishery—with small wary trout. In this water, an angler is happy with every trout seen, happier still with each trout taken, held, and released. A few small trout from a small stream will fill you with more wonder than a dozen leviathans taken from a super-fishery. There is no reason why this should be so (the tailwater trout are certainly no less beautiful), but it appears to be in our nature to take that which comes easily for granted. The fourteen-inch trout taken from a small stream, the monster that comes once a day if we are lucky, the trout that has been taken from water where only eight and ten-inch trout have been taken before—that trout is a monster, a behemoth, a wonder.

A. J. DeRosa, who guides all over the West and has a rich and broad perspective, has guided many anglers who fish the tailwaters almost exclusively. Tailwaters, he said, may be a wonderful place to hone technique (there is no substitute for numbers when learning to drift a fly or play a fish), to experiment with fly patterns, to work on the details of fishing mechanics, but there is something missing in this unique environment that the angler with broader experience senses immediately. He wondered what the trout fishing world must look like to one who has come to fishing as an adult, arrived in the stream a success in the world of business, or at least with enough money to begin his fishing life with the best equipment, on the best known water, with a guide to put him over trout, and provide a taking fly. What must he think of trout? A magnificent creature? A wild and wary animal? A difficult quarry? I doubt it.

Another good friend and guide, Bud Collins, says it a bit more bluntly: "They don't deserve these trout!"

This seems like arrogance, but Bud is a gentle and gracious man, an angler of prodigious talent, and truly humble. I know that Bud would prefer to teach people to fish on small streams, to allow a new angler to discover trout in an environment a little wilder than that of the tailwater. He would like to see a fisherman learn to drop a fly into a small pocket and keep it there drag free, to crouch and move carefully, to stalk each precious trout he is lucky enough to encounter. He would like to see a fisherman learn wonder and awe before he hauls in too many big trout. I would too.

I have spoken with a lot of anglers. There are things I want to know. There are issues that burn for me, and some of them are related to fishing. As much as I wonder why we are here, what it is that makes a child's eyes so beautiful, why it is that the company of an old friend can be so wonderful; I wonder too why each of us that has fished for a while seems to have a piece of water that we call home. And I wonder what it is that makes water assume that special status. For everyone the answers are different. I know that I, however, could never consider a tailwater my home stream.

A home stream, for me, must be in sight of the mountains. There must be the hope of alpenglow in the evening. A home stream must have trout, native trout. It must be wild and unregulated, flowing in accordance with the rhythms of nature—flooding when it rains hard or when the snow melts, slowing in the fall as it waits for winter and then another spring. A home stream must hold the promise of trout, but no guarantee that you will catch any. A home stream must be a place where you can go to find solitude. And it should be a place where you can be surprised to find that you are not alone. Deer should come to drink in the water that you fish and you should startle each other at least occasionally. Every now and then a bear should wander by at a distance, making your heart race. And, every now and then, you should run across another angler, one in whose company you feel immediately welcome, and with whom conversation is easy. A home stream should be a place, too, where you can come around a bend and see a child, crouched by a pool drifting a worm impaled on a hook through the water. A skinny, young arm should hold a stick to which a section of monofilament has been tied. The child should think he is alone, in a secret place in a secret wood. He should have walked to the stream or maybe ridden an old one-speed bike with balloon tires, and then carefully stashed it in the brush where the trail leaves the dirt road for the stream. The child's clothes should be serviceable, not fashionable, and worn (especially the knees). The child's eyes should be full of joy.

I've not seen these things on the tailwaters.

DAMN TROUT

Here it comes, more introspection on the subject of fishing. As surely as a hangover follows a binge, give an angler a minute to think and introspection will follow as if it were unavoidable. The fisherman becomes a helpless vehicle for the communication of some higher wisdom over which he has no control. Put an angler on a stream and his thoughts will inevitably turn from trout, caddis, midges, mayflies, and water; alder, willow, and cottonwood; red canyons, green hills, blue sky—to Nature, the Eternal Order, and the Meaning of Life.

A few years back I read an article by a Jungian psychologist who was intrigued by this phenomenon. I'm not sure exactly how I feel about Jungian psychology, but that isn't the real problem. What I resent is the tone of the article, a tone that insinuates something sinister—that fishing is more than recreation, that the act of fishing speaks about emptiness, an emptiness characterized by profound seeking, a dredging of the rivers and lakes in search of identity. He seemed to be saying that anglers—like anorexics, hand washers, door-knob wipers, string savers, child molesters, and other perverts—reveal more about who they are with their behavior than they would choose to if they had any choice in the matter, and further, that what they reveal is not good. Reading the article I felt as if a stranger had suddenly opened the bathroom door and caught me with my pants down. Always assuming that I had a great deal in common with Izaak Walton and Herman Melville, I was surprised to find that I was, in fact, working in the tradition of Philip Roth and Woody Allen.

Anglers are not the only people dedicated to their avocation. Joggers rise before dawn, to tie the laces of their hundred-dollar running shoes, to slip into Lycra tights with their eyes half closed in order to get in ten miles before breakfast. They become morbidly depressed when weather or injury prevent them from pounding their joints into oblivion. Gardeners I know spend all of their outdoor time on their knees, bent double, loving every minute of lower back pain, begrudging their erect moments because they are spent away from the weeds and the dirt. I have known model railroad devotees who disappear into shadowy, dank basements (after donning striped engineer's caps and bib overalls) to spend evening after evening in the company of spiders. They make miniature railroad stations and trestles with glue and balsa wood. They prepare grades, set ties, lay track, drive miniature spikes, and pour miniature ballast while recordings of steam locomotives chuffing upgrade roar in the background. Is this not obsessive? But who accuses them of dredging for identity? They are called hobbyists. Anglers, however, we know to be sick.

Fishermen, unfortunately, do nothing to protect themselves

from the accusation. If we simply spent absurd amounts of time fishing, tying flies, reading angling magazines and books, polishing and oiling reels, building rods, cleaning fly lines, and daydreaming about ten-pound browns taken in weedy water on 8X tippets knotted to #26 midges, if we simply wasted thousands of dollars flying to British Columbia to catch pneumonia in the cold rain all the while being told how great the fishing was last week ("too bad we haven't seen any fish this week"), then we would be simple hobbyists too; but we insist on going from the stream to eternity, from trout to the meaning of life at the drop of a soggy hat. I hate to admit it, but the diagnosis fits.

Once we discover how revealing this tendency toward metaphysics can be we try to hide it, but like all neurotic behavior, unless the root causes are uncovered and resolved, the symptoms reappear.

I've got a good friend and fishing buddy who was on a trip through the Grand Canyon with a bunch of city folks from Baltimore. They were the kind of people who see those of us who live in the San Juans as quaint guys with hay in our hair, smiling eyes and empty minds to match our empty days. And, of course, that's precisely what we want them to think. People don't bother you with too many questions if they assume you don't have any answers. Unfortunately guys like my friend Hollis have trouble keeping their mouths shut.

For the most part it was a pretty good trip. Hollis had rowed some rapids. He'd spent hours lying naked on the tubes of a rubber raft watching the sky and the layered canyon walls turn in lazy circles as the boats drifted through the calm stretches, as naked Baltimore women with flat stomachs and shaved legs lounged on the adjacent tubes. I imagine he did a pretty good job of appearing simple. Somewhere in the canyon, though, he lost it. It all started the evening he was standing in Havasu Falls, taking a shower—a wash rag in one hand, a fishing pole in the other. The day's memories were fresh and they were all good. A beautiful blue sky, sheer canyon walls, and wild water framed his vision; thoughts about time, permanence, and impermanence floated from unconscious genetic memory into the consciousness of introspection; beer lubricated his thought. Still, his mouth remained shut. But in the shower, with a washrag wrapped around his future and his free hand gripping the swollen corks of a fiberglass rod, fishing as he bathed (a Jungian psychotherapist's quintessential metaphor), a trout struck. And what a trout it turned out to be, five pounds if it was an ounce, wild, strong.

"By God, this is what it's all about! Life flows like a big, wild river, framed in beauty, filled with adventure, inhabited by creatures whose very nature and destiny reflect the character of their surroundings. The common basis of humankind's quest for meaning, the hopes of that quest codified in religious tradition, the contents expressed in our aesthetic products—visual art, dance, music, theater, literature—and the meaning we glean from the flow of events and call history, all here in these two rods and their throb, in the creature at the end of my fishing rod and the woman who isn't at the end of the other! Life by God, LIFE!"

The silence had been broken.

Next day, drifting through a calm stretch, a university professor in the group turned to Hollis and said, "You know, I think I owe you an apology. I had you figured all wrong. When I first met you I thought you were some kind of hick, but the fact of the matter is, you're an intellectual."

The words struck Hollis like a blow from the blind side. He'd been prepared for big water, hot weather, warm beer, scorpions, and snakes, but this? This *insult?* What could he do, how should he respond? He did what he had to do, what he wanted to do, and what he couldn't keep himself from doing—he laid the guy out with a right and swore in a soft, venomous whisper, as full of malice as any sound he had ever made as the professor watched wide-eyed and stunned from the rippling rubber bottom of the raft, "If you ever talk to me like that again, I swear I'll kill you."

But the damage had been done.

He knows it, and I know it, and it doesn't do any good to talk about it. If it hadn't been for that goddamn trout only a few good friends would ever have known that a bit of John Dewey, some Sam Clemens, and more than a little Dickens reside behind those clear eyes with the laugh lines around the edges.

It's my guess that the professor amuses his friends in fern bars by the harbor of Baltimore with stories about the mountain boy on the river, about his great sensitivity to the beauty and meaning of nature. The mountain boy with the silver tongue, and the wise heart. Damn trout.

DOLORES IS STILL DANCING

I know that all of us who live in the shadow of the San Juans share something, but I'm not sure what it is. Is it just the place or is there something more? More than a few of my friends from elsewhere have observed that the thing we share is readily apparent: we're all nuts. In the hope of clarifying that observation I bring to you now my dear friend Dolores. A typical San Juaner, by virtue of not being typical.

Dolores once asked me to do a photograph for a story Ray Mungo was writing for *New Age* magazine. Although she was known to a large number of underground environmentalists and monkey-wrenchers, an assortment of Tai Chi dancers, and a vast network of deep ecology, bio-regional, re-inhabitory, ritual-devolutionary cohorts, she had certainly not achieved the kind of general notoriety that would make her name a household word. Mungo's piece, I hoped, would broaden her recognition, and the illustrating photograph had to capture and communicate her spirit.

It was the late seventies, and Ray Mungo was still somewhat notorious from his days at the Liberation News Service. The reporters of the Liberation News Service were young journalists, mostly college students, who tried in the sixties to give us an alternative to the fraudulent body counts and glowing stories of Green Berets winning the hearts and minds of the Vietnamese people that filled the mainstream press. Radicals, hated by most Americans, people like Mungo were never again a part of the American mainstream (even though their dedication to getting the other side of the news into print was vindicated by the facts, when finally some of the facts became known). I suspect that's the way Ray wanted it.

He wrote a novel about wisdom and the Far East (*Return to Sender*) that poked fun at the tendency to look for wisdom in meditation and separation from the real world. A political creature always, Mungo believed (even in the New Age) that enlightenment was not found in herbs, spices, and mystical separation. He found in Dolores LaChapelle a mentor and a colleague.

Dolores' wisdom has always been attractive to crystal-wielders and New Agers, but she is not one of them. Her philosophy, her action, are rooted in place, and wed to the very real earth. The perfect bridge between Mungo's occidental politicism and the New Age's vaguely oriental mysticism, Dolores was an appropriate subject for him and for this magazine.

A perfect subject, perhaps, but awfully hard to classify. Included in most anthologies that concern radical environmentalism (or more specifically, deep ecology) Dolores' writing defies description. Claimed by eco-feminists as one of the sisterhood, she rejects the association; yet she lives to embody many eco-feminist ideals. She is a strong woman who takes crap from no one. She sees the very real difference between the way men live and relate to the earth and the way woman do. Yet she can easily say, "eco-feminism is a problem and not a solution." Sometimes, when they know her better, eco-feminists become angry with her and reject her utterly. Her solidarity is with the earth, and not with environmentalists—women or men.

She lectures, she writes, she leads rituals, but none of this is my experience of her. These things make me nervous. I know her as a friend and as a woman who is extraordinary company in the mountains. There is a saying that goes, "You've gotta walk your talk." Dolores walks it best above timberline, on the tundra and steep rock, or in the trees when the snow is deep and gravity is pulling her down, skis dancing beneath her feet as she snakes through the timber.

The first time I saw Dolores she was dancing in the powder on Kendall Mountain, above Silverton. I had gone to look for a place to live. The publishing company for which I had been working in Denver was planning a move to the San Juans the following spring. I would be returning to the mountains to live in the spring and I needed to find a house. My wife and I spent Christmas vacation there, looking around and cross country skiing. One day, while plodding up the slopes of Kendall Mountain on cross-country skis we watched as two figures cut beautiful turns through the snow above us. When they reached us, they stopped and said hello. It was Dolores and her husband, Ed. We talked for a while, were invited to dinner that evening, then watched as they skied down the mountain. Someday, I thought, I'd like to ski like that.

Dolores adopted me the next winter. It was the drought year of '76–'77. Although there was little snow at the ski areas, snow did fall in sufficient depths to ski up high in the backcountry. It stayed light and untracked on sheltered slopes above timberline, and it lasted in the trees near timberline between the widely spaced storms. All winter we climbed together and we skied together. One day. One climb. One run.

Dolores learned to ski as a teenager in 1943. She and her sister would ride west from Denver to Loveland Pass in a truck full of Colorado Mountain Club junior members. The Juniors' truck had been used for ski trips before the war and therefore had been granted a gasoline ration. The ration, however, was only sufficient for trips to and from the pass. There was not enough gas to take the young skiers up and down the mountain during their days of skiing. Because of this, the truck would deposit the group above old Highway 6 at the Zipfelberger Hut, where they would listen for other trucks grinding their way up the pass. When they heard one coming up the road, they'd race down to the highway from the hut, wait for the truck to come by, and hope that the driver would stop and give them a lift to the top. Once they had made it to the top they would strap on their skis and ski through the powder back down to the hut, where they would wait for another truck and repeat the process until dark descended.

Dolores continued to ski after the war in Aspen where she took a job as a schoolteacher. Later, after meeting Ed on a Canadian climbing expedition, they married and she moved with him to Alta, Utah, where he did avalanche research and she continued to ski.

She knows snow. I remember skiing behind her in the backcountry, laboring in the deep powder. The army surplus climbing skins she loaned me were strapped to long black Head Standard skis that had free-heel cable bindings. Her own skis were Miller Softs with the same Silveretta binding. Our binding hinges would squeak as we climbed. Over the sound of my own labored breathing I could hear her speaking.

"Look at that cliff!" she would say. "It sticks out there like a Japanese scroll!" And it did. "Why is it that we insist on looking at the Japanese as Buddhist; that's crazy, their roots are Shinto. It's in their art. It's in their lives." And I supposed that this too was true. As true as the fact of the cliff.

"See that dull, satin sheen on the snow up there?" I did. "Bad news, that's wind slab. Hard, dangerous stuff, we'd better get away from it." From a mile off she could see the snow and know what it would be like. She'd poke the snow with her pole on the way up, along the track she was making, around the bases of trees. "Depth hoar. These trees will eat you up. Stay away from them on the way down." I listened

And on the way down I followed. Dolores didn't teach skiing by way of lecture. She moved. On a slope of steady pitch, she would rise up after a pole plant and roll her knees, the snow would turn her skis, she'd sink down into the snow and wait for the pressure to build, finishing the turn, then the snow would release her skis and she'd rise again. The track this movement of body and skis would make in the snow would be a series of tight, round turns in the powder. On rolling terrain, or over cornices and steep drops, she would rise up and spread her arms, like a soaring bird, making a wide arc over the drop, and if you followed her you would feel that you were flying. After a season of follow ing in her tracks I found that I felt a little of what she felt when she skied. I turned where she turned. To this day, if we ski down a slope beside each other, only peripherally aware that we are skiing side by side, at the end of the run we will look up and marvel at the fact that our turns came in the same places. At least I will marvel. It makes perfect sense to Dolores. "Well, of course, we turned when the mountain told us."

There are no speeches when Dolores skis. Only bliss. For-give the use of such a strong word, but it is the only one I know that applies. Shinto is forgotten, Buddhism a distant annoyance.

Ideas of place disappear in the experience of place itself, in the experience of snow and gravity and mountains, and Dolores becomes a little girl playing in the snow.

There is an intellectual side to Dolores that is a bit unnerving. She graduated Phi Beta Kappa from the University of Denver, but that seems like irrelevant, ancient history. The ideas and information that fill her mind today come from the voluminous reading she does in historical Asian thought, worldwide indigenous culture and ritual, contemporary thought both Western and Eastern, her conversations with her impressive circle of friends in the world of professional philosophy, and, more significantly, from her intimate experience with and keen observations of nature. To a linear thinker it is disconcerting to go from the phenomenon of the glory (a 360-degree rainbow with the viewer in the center that can be seen from mountain summits and airplanes) to the origins of religion, but this is the kind of jump she makes without hesitation. There is an arrogance that seems, at times, appalling. I once heard her say, "No one in the West understands Shinto as well as I do." But these, I have come to realize, are momentary outbursts of zeal, enthusiasm. It is the same arrogance that allows a painter to race across canvas with confidence. The self-doubt comes later. Had it come to edit there would have been no painting, and there would be no Dolores.

As extreme as her case might be, I find in Dolores the perfect example of one who has found a home in the San Juans. To some, she is merely the proof of a joke a good friend of mine once made. "San Juan County," Hollis had said with the certainty of one who had been there, "is the world's largest open-air asylum." Its inhabitants, he implied, were all crazy. There is more than a little truth in that.

Some would like to excuse the long-time mining families from this indictment. They, it might be argued, were born here.

We transplants moved here. Our insanity is demonstrated in an act of the will. Yet the miners who stay profess a love for the place, and there are certainly easier ways to make a living. For all who choose to stay there is a choice. We were all refugees in the asylum.

Another friend, one who has long since left San Juan County for a different kind of isolation in the New Mexico desert, said it differently. "The county isn't so much an asylum as a Zen monastery. People go there to learn something, and when they learn it they leave." Nelson now lives in a sun-warmed adobe beside the Rio Grande River below Taos.

Mary Swanson ran a grocery store on Blair Street for many years. She was a woman who had seen much of her family wiped out in the flu epidemic of 1918. Thrust into the roles of mother and father by the deaths of both her parents, she became the matriarch of a clan that has had a significant impact on the history of San Juan County. That is not why I mention her here. It is the way residents describe the place that intrigues me at the moment, and the way the descriptions vary yet remain similar.

Mary didn't move to Silverton from an eastern city. She lived in the mountains all her life. I once asked her if she knew of anyone else who had experienced the San Juans as I had—had seen them and known that someday they would return there to live. "Oh yes," she replied, "it is the magnet of the mountains. Some cannot resist their pull. Some who feel it try to leave, for jobs, for love of someone who cannot live here, but the mountains always pull them back."

These are strange descriptions. This is a place that is thought of for its incredible scenic beauty. Coffee table books on the Rockies and scenic calendars are full of pictures of its more accessible ranges and easily photographed mountains—the Grenadiers from Molas Lake, the Sneffels Range from Dallas Divide, Grizzly Peak from Jarvis Meadows. "Asylum," "monastery," and "magnet" are not the words that I would have come up with had I only seen them in books and calendars, had I never lived in their midst.

Dolores recently had her old house razed and another built in its place. She told me a story about the day the old house came down. A woman called from Princeton, New Jersey. She was the editor of the newsletter that is produced by the Pagan Branch of the Unitarian Church. She wanted some advice, some information, and to order a book. In the middle of the phone call Dolores blurted out, "I can't talk right now, the bulldozer is knocking my wall down." And she hung up, without explanation.

The old house had to come down if Dolores were to stay in the mountains. It had drains that froze every winter. They froze early if the snow came late and failed to insulate the ground. They froze later, even when the snows fell early and deep. Sooner or later they always froze. The toilet continued to flush, but the sinks and the shower would not drain. Gophers were undermining the foundation. The insulation was marginal. In a town where thirty-five degrees below zero is not uncommon, Dolores slept in a bedroom that was the same temperature as the valley outside by the time morning came. I remember one night in 1976 when my thermometer went down to forty below where the marks ended, and then continued to drop; a night when frost formed on the inside walls of my insulated house. Dolores had a good sleeping bag.

Dolores didn't worry so much about her own comfort, but she worried about her plants when she was away. She worried about the people who came to visit, even though they smiled as they shivered in the morning, not wanting to admit their discomfort as their cold hands cradled warm cups of barley water and they pressed their frozen rumps against the hot metal of the rekindled earth stove. I think she sometimes worried about me. The first time I spent the night at Dolores' house I made the mistake of trying to take a shower in the morning—and I ended up with pneumonia.

The new house is solar. It is insulated. It holds the heat of the high altitude sun, the heat so generously given even during the depths of the winter, and it holds that heat through the cold night. Her drains flow and her bedroom never gets down to forty below any more. Above the kitchen she has built a warm, cozy loft for those who visit her—pagans, vegetarians, the meat-eating cowboys who built her house and are now her friends, ski bums, professional philosophers, wide-eyed innocents, and wise old men and women. She spent nearly every penny she had to build the new house. It is a commitment to place, to her belief that she could not live anywhere else.

"People leave here for better weather. They leave for better jobs. They think they'll be happy, but they don't realize until they're gone how much they will miss the light, the high altitude light. They can replace the mountains with the sea, maybe. They can find isolation if they want it. But they can never replace this light. That's why I built the house. I can't live anyplace else."

The photograph I delivered to Mungo shows Dolores doing Tai Chi on a rock above an abyss. The distant canyon walls below and behind her are in shadow, nearly black. She stands, semi-crouched, with one hand pointing into the rock at her feet, the other held away from her body, open, toward the sun. A long braid flows from her head to her waist. She is bathed in the high altitude light she loves so much. She is dancing. Dolores is still dancing.

DRIFTING

Bonita Peak rises above the tundra, its 13,286-foot summit visible from much of the high country of San Juan County. It looks massive and immutable, immune to human enterprise, but looks can be deceiving. Much of the mountain has been hollowed out, ground into powder and deposited as mill tailings in the valley floor, or hauled off as precious metal concentrate to smelters in Texas. The mountain, so solid when seen from afar, is honeycombed with the workings of the Sunnyside Mine. In the engineering office of the mine, on the blueprints that detail the guts of Bonita Peak, the mountain seems on the verge of collapse. Things aren't always what they appear to be.

It was just a matter of time before the desire to live in the mountains and the reality of paying the bills led me into the Sunnyside Mine. When I came to the San Juans with the publishing company that was relocating from Denver, I really didn't think the firm would last very long in Silverton. The owner had always imagined his business operating from a small mountain town and he jumped at the opportunity to move to the mountains when the San Juan County Historical Society offered him the old Denver & Rio Grande Western railroad depot in Silverton, rent free, if he would fix it up. It was a lot harder, however, for him to leave Denver where he had been born, gone through school, and spent his young adulthood than he ever could have imagined. A lot of city people have romantic visions of mountain life and move to small towns like Silverton full of eagerness and joy. After a few winters battling broken pipes, fly ash, and cabin fever, after spending one too many evenings alone, he moved back to the city of his birth.

My desire to be in the San Juans was as full of illusions and romanticism as his, but time here changed me. Although I too had to deal with the broken pipes, the constant cutting and splitting of wood for the stove, the fear that I hadn't gathered enough to make it through the winter, although I too suffered my share of cabin fever, there was more for me here than hardship. I loved the short but brilliant days of winter. I used the long nights to advantage, preparing photographs for exhibition, spending time in the company of friends, or reading. I found that I loved to ski—and that more than anything else redeemed the long winter. The publisher returned to Denver after a few years, taking his company and my job with him. I stayed behind.

With the exception of a few year-round businesses, the state highway department, and city and county government there are two kinds of jobs in San Juan County: mining and tourism. Selling hamburgers and rubber tomahawks to tourists is a summer occupation and I needed a more reliable occupation when the publisher departed. Mining seemed the way to go. Just as the warmth of summer inevitably passes and slides through fall into the long night of winter, I moved, inexorably, from publishing into the mine.

I was hired as an electrician by the head sparky. We had worked together rewiring the old depot. We had been colleagues in publishing together in Denver and during our first year in the mountains. After the remodeling of the old depot had been completed, he had a falling out with our employer and went to work in the mine. I followed him into the mine, about a year later.

A good friend, a lady who was a certified hoistman and had been working underground for quite some time, told me that I wouldn't know how I was going to react to being underground until I got there. Some panic, some are simply uncomfortable, she said. Others work as they would anywhere else, apparently oblivious to the fact that they are thousands of feet from the surface of the earth, buried alive inside a mountain. A few actually love the place and thrive there as nowhere else, feeling truly alive only when surrounded by tunnels of rock and the steady dripping of underground water, in the presence of gold.

The first day on the job, my diggers were clean and marked me as a new man. The rubberized nylon bib and jacket glowed bright yellow without the gray-brown stains of muck and blasting powder. My steel-toed rubber boots had no leaks and still kept the water out. My mind was as innocent of underground stains as my protective clothing. I hadn't known anyone who had fallen dead in the bad air that lingers after a blast. I hadn't known anyone who had been electrocuted by a stray wire or decapitated by a timber carried on the deck of a locomotive through a portal too narrow to allow its passage. I could not know on my first day underground that each of these horrors, and many more, would occur during my tenure in the mine, but I knew mining was dangerous.

Each day every miner was reminded of that fact, if not by

the work itself then by the Fatalgrams that papered the wall on the way to the mantrip. Fatalgrams are posterlike announcements of fatal accidents, with illustrations of the accident scenes and photographs of the mangled corpses (when there were enough pieces to be photographed) of miners who have died in recent mining accidents. They are distributed by the Mine Safety and Health Administration in the hope that exposure to the grotesque consequences of unsafe mining practices will induce safe work habits. The trip into the mine began with a walk through a tunnel, past the Fatalgrams, and into the cars of the tiny train known as the mantrip that hauled us from the portal in Gladstone to Main Level Station two miles inside the mountain.

Around me on the mantrip sat about fifty men and a few women, some of whom had worked as miners all of their working lives. Most of the miners had been raised by fathers who had been miners. Some of the mining crews consisted of brothers. Others were made up of lifelong friends who had been born in the mountains, grown up in Silverton, played basketball together for The Silverton Miners in High School, and subsequently graduated to a real mining team, and left the gym for the underground tunnels and stopes of the Sunnyside Mine. Many on that train could not imagine any other life.

We were sitting in squat, cold, yellow cars. Steel benches faced each other at a distance of about eighteen inches. Miners on opposing benches placed their legs so that they alternated with the legs of those across from them. Between your own legs was the leg of another, and each of your knees rode in the crotch of a fellow miner. Beside you sat two others clad in rubber, their shoulders pressed against yours. The sheet metal of the car roof hovered inches above each head. I thought of the diagrams I had seen of slave ships, diagrams that outlined a meticulous use of space, that wasted nothing, save perhaps human comfort and dignity. Each head was covered with a broad-brimmed, brown hardhat that looked very much like a World War I doughboy's helmet. From a wet-cell battery belted to each waist a cable ran up the back, over the helmet, to a clamp that held a lamp. On many of the hardhats there were hatbands made from sections of automobile tire inner tube. Stuck in the bands were the red and yellow crayons that were used to mark the rock for drilling. Mud-splattered safety glasses dangled below each chin, suspended by a single earpiece; the other earpiece hung free.

As the mantrip jerked to a start and rolled away from the portal, I glanced toward the face of the man on my left. He was scratching under his long mustache in the several days old stubble of his chin with the nubs of fingers that had once populated his hand. His fingers had long ago been lost between steel and rock while wrestling an unruly drill. As the portal receded, miners switched off their lights and snatched a few minutes rest. It was totally dark, except for the lamp of the hoistman. She was staring absent-mindedly at the rock ribs of the tunnel, rock ribs that came into view as the mantrip pulled away from the metal sets of the portal and along which her lamp light played as the mantrip continued its bumpy journey into the diggings. Turning to me with eyes wide and glowing in the dim light, she whispered, "Isn't the rock beautiful?"

The structure of a mine is complex, but the purpose is simple. Every tunnel, every hole, each piece of rail, every machine is there to accomplish one task: to bring ore-bearing rock to the surface. The community that supports this purpose is organized hierarchically and the social structure of a mine reflects that hierarchy. The miners are preeminent. Everyone else in the mine is there to serve them. Slusherman move broken rock out of their way, so they can work (or pull the broken rock they have left behind into ore chutes). Trammers haul the ore around the mine and out of the portal in trains. Nippers move supplies in and out of the mine. Timberman construct hoists and shore up weak walls. Mechanics and machine doctors keep the equipment working. Hoistman and tugger operators move people and equipment up and down in the mine. The shit-nipper cleans the latrines. Geologists and engineers come in from the office every now and then to get their diggers dirty, and electricians, at the bottom of the heap, replace light bulbs. At least that's what one miner told me.

The miners, too, had a pecking order. The best contracts involved working the veins of high-grade ore in large excavations known as stopes. Drilling in support of stopes was less glamorous and less lucrative. Those who drilled the tunnels that wound through waste rock were called "drifters"; the tunnels they drilled were called "drifts."

Although the pecking order was clear, everyone who worked underground was bound to everyone else. In a town that lived or died as mining prospered or failed, anyone who went underground was a little special. Each time someone died, we remembered why.

The Lead Electrician on my shift was a tall scraggly conservative Republican. He'd have preferred John Wayne or Barry Goldwater in the White House, but must have been happy years later when Ronald Reagan was swept into the Presidency on a cresting wave of patriotic sentiment (or nostalgia for old movies). He appeared to be about fifty or sixty years old. In fact, he was scarcely forty. I don't think it was the mining that aged him. It was the liquor.

I watched him one evening after day shift and a few hours in the bar, as he tried to insert a key into the lock of his front door. From a distance of about a foot he would lift his right hand (the one holding the key) and move it toward the lock. As his hand neared the keyhole, he would lose his balance and stagger backward a few steps. Slowly he would gather his balance, walk forward, and try again. Over and over he repeated the sequence. I can only imagine the bad dream that was playing in his head. I can't tell you how long this went on, because I got tired of watching after about fifteen minutes. There was no point in offering to help—it would have been an insult—so I went about my business. In the morning, smoke was rising from his chimney, indicating that he had managed to get the door open without my help.

A Lead Electrician is supposed to show a new man around. I thought this meant teaching me where to find tools and parts, how to find my way in the complexity of tunnels, and how to get the work done. On my first shift he taught me where the shitters were (small shacks in the mine with good old-fashioned one-holers), how to get into the Old Sunnyside workings through a breach in the rib of a drift on F-Level ("in case you wanna do some exploring"). He also introduced me to my partner—a guy I already knew pretty well, whose trademark was that he never walked a drift without singing a Tom Lehrer song—"First you get down on your knees, fiddle with your rosaries . . ."

I worked in that hole in the ground for about a year before finding infinitely more pleasure working in the company of cowboys, cottonmouths, copperheads, and irate property owners in the swamps of East Texas—and it's a good thing I did. It's not that I didn't like the people in the mine. To this day, some of those I am likely to spend a day with in the woods or on a stream are friends I made in the mine (including one who tried to blow up the electrician's shop with a case of powder—but that's another story); rather, it's because I prefer sweating in a swamp where I can see the sky, feel the sun, and breathe fresh air, to spending my days living like a mole. The reason it was a good thing that I ended up in Texas transcends my desire to work above ground. While I was up to my neck in swamp water, about a week after leaving the mine, the roof of a stope that had been worked a little too close up under Lake Emma (which sat none too far above the rock ceilings of the stopes on C-Level) gave way, flushing the Sunnyside with millions of gallons of frigid, murky, alpine lake water. Nobody died because the cave-in occurred on a Sunday night, the only shift during which the mine was empty. But it was a disaster nonetheless. Nearly everyone was laid off until management could survey the damage, and in the year or so it took to get things going again it seemed as if the Great Depression had returned to San Juan County.

A lot of people, not born into mining families, came and went from the mine in the years before the cave-in. They still come and go. Some are urban refugees looking for a way to make a living in the mountains. Some are tramp miners who go from town to town looking for a mine that is hiring, leaving behind one that is laying off. The real miners in San Juan County are hard working family men who stay with it for a long time, doing a hard job and doing it well. These are the guys who worked the stopes. The rest of the people in the mine were mostly drifting.

The singing sparky left his wife and kids for a pretty young blond from Durango. Together, they went off to Pennsylvania. His kids stayed behind with their mother. I've never known two tougher kids. The boy broke his leg a few years back when a school bus in Durango lost its footing on an icy road and plunged down a canyon into the Animas River. I wasn't there, but I imagine him tying off the bleeding leg with his bandana and cussing a blue streak at anyone who tried to touch him. His little sister, by the way, was even tougher. His wife got shot in a domestic dispute a few years after he left her, and died. The tall, gray Republican electrician was working in yet another hole in the ground near Fairplay, Colorado, last I heard. He was the one who told me about the shooting and I remember thinking how hollow his eyes looked as he spoke—hollow, like the insides of Bonita Peak.

About as close as I get to Bonita Peak any more is across the valley when I go up to the Highland Mary Lakes or over the High Divide to fish Pole Creek and the Rio Grande headwaters. From the neighborhood of these lakes, these streams—a world as lush and brilliant as the Sunnyside Mine is sterile and dark—Bonita Peak looks pretty solid. Having been in the mine, I know better. It's not just mining in San Juan County that's given me that perspective. I like to think that fishing has helped a bit too. I once worked in an office in New York City and I'm not sure if the mine was any darker. Fishing taught me that.

SMYTHE

Smythe was not like the rest of us—not like anyone that most of us had ever known. He was a loner, but that was common in the San Juans, and it was not his desire for privacy that made him so different. Smythe lived among us with an intensity that was tangible, sometimes frightening. As different as he was, none of us ever thought of him as anything other than a member of the community. I sometimes think that his story, the story of his time in the San Juans, says as much about the people as anything I remember. The story of his sad demise and how we reacted says something, too.

I've heard a great deal from folks who have never lived in a rural area—in the West, in the mountains—that although the beauty is compelling and they love to come here to recharge their emotional batteries,

87

they could never actually live in such a place. The people are just a bit too crude for their tastes, a bit too parochial.

There's some truth in these observations. Rural people wear their insecurities on their sleeves for everyone to see; it often seems that the more remote, the more isolated the community, the more the inhabitants feel the need to apologize for their home. This is coupled with a strangely contradictory sense of pride in being able to live, and survive, in such a place. If the place is rugged, the weather harsh, then this tendency is magnified. The fear, the apology, and the pride breed another apparently common rural trait—mistrust of anyone from somewhere else.

If I had to generalize (an always dangerous proposition) I'd say that Westerners tend to dislike authority and everything associated with it. Easterners, it seems, are more likely to accept rules. Even a simple thing like the zoning of land is seen in the West as tyranny, the product of overzealous government. In the East, such things have been established for so long that they are no longer the cause of outrage. Maybe the western attitude remains from a not too distant time when both law and government were far away and people had to settle their differences without help. Maybe the West has always attracted a disproportionate number of people who wanted to get away from structure of any kind. Maybe the attraction of the West—of the broad expanse of sky, of the isolation of living in a world that is circumscribed by high, protective peaks—is partly the attraction of separation from authority.

Whether this stereotype is valid or not, there has always been a presumption that those who choose isolation also choose to distrust anything or anyone that comes to remind them of the things they left behind. This is one cause of the proverbial redneck. This is one reason for those awkward moments when a stranger walks into a small town cafe looking for a cup of coffee and every head pivots, every eye stares at the stranger, silently, and with suspicion.

Or so we imagine, when we imagine such an encounter.

I have experienced such things when traveling the West. Once I walked into a coffee shop off the main highway in eastern Oregon, road weary and buzzing with vibration from having squeezed the steering wheel for a couple hundred miles as wind-drifted snow alternated with brilliant blue sky and the road changed suddenly from black to white without warning. I wanted a friendly moment with a few people and a cup of coffee. What I found was a surly waitress who could not manage a smile or a kind word. What I found was a counter filled with silent men, men drinking coffee in the middle of the day as a bitter cold wind blew desiccated snow horizontally past the cafe windows. I found men who were trapped in the cafe by the weather and the lack of work, and I supposed that they presumed I was not one of them because my car was not a truck and because it was filled with the luggage and rod tubes of a vacationing angler. They had no desire to be friendly. I drank my coffee in silence and went back to the manageable hostility of the road.

It happened to me the winter I came to Silverton looking for a place to live. I walked into the Best Cafe for coffee on a December day when the sun shone with a brilliance that hurt and the morning air was so cold it burned. I opened the door to the cafe, walked in, and saw the backs of people drinking coffee at the counter. In unison their heads turned toward me and I saw eyes filled with distrust. The room was silent. In that instant I knew them to be narrow-minded, suspicious, and hostile. I wondered if the mountains would ever bring me enough solace to compensate me for the manners of the locals.

Smythe was gay. I don't know if there is anything I would have expected to inflame a narrow-minded person, a redneck, like homosexuality. Nothing, I would have thought, would have outraged a parochial populace more, except maybe the communists thought to be hiding behind the bushes. But such was not the case. When I first moved to Silverton, the librarian was a lesbian and her long-time companion was a tugger operator at the mine. Both women were well integrated into the social fabric of the town, liked by most, unliked by some, but the fact of their sexual preferences seemed to have little to do with it.

Smythe was a writer. He tried to make a living doing free-lance journalism, but like the rest of us, sooner or later he knew he'd end up working for the mining company. Eventually it became his lot to take a place in the mill, working a shovel, picking up muck that had fallen from the conveyor. He worked beside the roaring belts, the screeching rollers, the falling rock. He kept his soul alive by writing fiction that hid in reams tucked away in his room. He was always writing. He shoveled half-heartedly because his mind was composing careful sentences. In the bar he took notes. On the street he would stop to pull a pad from his pocket to record an observation.

Before he went to work in the mill he tried his hand at surveying, which is how I first got to know him. I had long since left the mine for a job with a survey crew. The crew I was with needed a rod man for a mapping project in the Utah desert near Dead Horse Point. Smythe needed work and he told me so one night over a beer. I called the crew chief, Smythe was hired, and a few days later we bounced off into the desert in my old green '63 GMC, V6 pickup.

A rod man isn't exactly a surveyor. On a survey crew he occupies a position somewhere between gopher and instrument man. His work isn't terribly demanding, but it is important. He has to find a place that isn't too high above or too far below the instrument. If he's smart, he can find such a place a good distance from the gun and he will make the miles pass quickly with long shots. He has to locate or create a turning point on which the rod can rotate without changing elevation. He has to watch the instrument man for signals that enable him to move the rod so that the man on the gun can see it properly. And he has to hold his point for two shots. More than anything else, he has to hold his point for two shots. If he loses the point between shots, everything that has been done by the crew before closing at the final benchmark will be lost.

Land that needs to be surveyed is, for some reason, always difficult. There is a variation of Murphy's Law that operates, but I haven't quite figured it out—if land isn't accurately mapped, maybe there's a reason; if an instrument doesn't like dust, it will be dusty; the shortest distance between two points always crosses a chasm. Maybe the most pertinent law is this: when it would be lethal for your mind to wander, your mind will wander. At any rate, one who was unaware of the consequences of this law, one who didn't live in constant fear of the wandering mind, one too new to surveying to tremble at the prospect would be sure to fall victim.

Smythe joined us for the inevitable. We needed an elevation several miles into the desert along a route that had no road, across terrain that yielded no easy path, on a day that reminded us that one of the great benefits of the mountains in summer is their ability to rise above the heat of the surrounding deserts. We were no longer in the mountains.

We began at a remote benchmark beside a dirt road far from asphalt, and worked our way on foot across the rock, the sand, and the widely scattered clumps of desert grasses. Hours passed for the three of us—two rod men and an instrument man— sighting the rod ahead, leapfrogging the rod man to shoot back at the turning point, motioning the rod man to move ahead, making the new shot, and so on. The work had a rhythm. The day absorbed it into itself along with the sun, the sand, and the wind. The two of us who had done it before fell into a wonderful state of intense awareness of the place, the details of the work, the ebb and flow of distractions from that work—it was, as always, a lot like meditation. But not for Smythe.

Smythe found his spots, he held his rod, he walked ahead when signaled to do so, but in the slack moments, the many minutes that grew into hours between those when the gun was focused on his rod, between those when he was walking to a new turning point, his pad was out and he was writing.

I suspect he was writing about the place. I suspect he was writing about the people with whom he worked—the strangely quiet cowboys wearing black hats in the blistering sun. I have hoped that he was writing about the obvious bond that had formed between the two regulars on the crew, Danny and I, who had repeated this routine together many times, in deserts, mountains, and swamps. I'll never know what he wrote. None of his prose other than newspaper stories ever came to light. Besides, any concern about what he might have been writing evaporated when, after five hours of walking in the desert, holding the rods, focusing the gun, and making sure that the sights would be accurate enough to close the work within tolerance so that this difficult march would never have to be repeated, Smythe picked up his rod too soon and began to walk. He walked after putting away his pad and scribbling a few notes. He walked after only one shot. The work, and the day, were lost.

Smythe was fired that evening and a few weeks later he was working a shovel at the mill. While there he uncovered a lot of information about the management of the mine. He predicted the demise of the workings unless something were done to correct many flagrant abuses. He wrote as if to prove Mark Twain's dictum, "A mine is a hole in the ground with a liar for an owner." He shared his thoughts with the locals and, largely because of that, he was fired from the mill. Having no way to earn a living, he was forced to leave the San Juans.

I didn't hear much about him for many years, but one day, sitting in a restaurant in Durango, I stumbled upon the current issue of the *Silverton Standard* and opened to a page that carried his obituary. He had died of AIDS in San Francisco after pursuing a career as a journalist. His story about the mine had been purchased by a big city paper but it never ran. Someone from the mining company had gotten to the editor. A friend of Smythe's told me that this embittered him. The mine went bankrupt a few years after he left. It now sits empty, the water dripping in huge, empty chasms that had been worked without regard for the future, in chasms that had been created when high-grade ore had been pulled prematurely in order to make a fast buck, in chasms that block access to future development of the mine. There are no miners in the mines of Silverton any more, only the steady dripping of water in the empty tunnels that Smythe wrote about before he left town. Before he became ill. Before he died.

The obituary had been written by the town's excellent historian, the curator of the Historical Society archives, the county judge, Allen Nossaman. It was long and respectful. It spoke of his family that grieved for him. It spoke of his time in Silverton as a writer and millhand. It spoke of him with kindness and it was read in kindness by those who remembered him. They talked about him with respect on the stools at the cafe in Silverton. They lamented the sad demise of the quiet man who had tried to uncover the problems at the mine, only to be run off by a greedy and inept mining corporation. They only stopped talking to be silent when a stranger walked in for a cup of coffee. Because the stranger might not understand how a gay man could have been such an important piece of the complex tapestry that is this remote little town. Because strangers always look at us funny when they walk into the cafe for a minute or two, before returning to their cars to drive back to the city.

A HAT FULL OF GOLD

It's a terrible thing to begin with a lie, but I console myself by thinking that there is a difference between a substantial lie and an alteration intended for a good purpose. The Catholic Church seems to have had this sort of thing in mind when it differentiated between the venal and the mortal. At any rate, this story about Chet isn't really about Chet, and many of the other facts are wrong too. Not wrong, really, just changed slightly. The reason is that Chet is a fiercely private man and he probably wouldn't want the world to know his business. In story-telling as in life it isn't the facts, so much, that matter, as the meaning. We've all read fishing stories where the author has changed the name of the stream to protect the identity of a fragile place. We don't consider that a lie. Let's say I'm trying to protect the identity of an equally fragile place. This private stream flows within a tough but fragile man and I would hate to see him bothered.

Chet was raised in the southern Rockies, but he's moved around a lot. He was born in the mountains of northern New Mexico, where he worked cattle from childhood. He cowboyed some as a young adult in California. In his late twenties he moved to the San Juans, where he continued to work cattle and, later, to wrangle horses for dudes. I met him in a bar in Silverton. His stories captivated me. I suppose the most extraordinary thing was the fact that he had no idea just how extraordinary he was. His life was his life and it seemed perfectly normal to him.

Chet was a fisherman and we spent a lot of time together poking about the high country lakes. We had a kind of symbiosis on fishing trips. He had horses, I tied flies. It worked pretty well. Together we could cover a lot of ground and a lot of fish.

But fishing was not his primary interest. Like many others in the San Juans his passion was gold.

A man is a strange assortment of things—muscles, sinew, viscera, ideas, and habits. Some things we are born with, others are absorbed from our culture and place. Chet is a man of the West and his heritage is uniquely Western.

A few years back Chet spent a few weeks in jail for assault. It wasn't really his fault, and he did his time quietly and in good humor. After all, he was there because he'd done the right thing.

A friend with whom he'd worked over the years owned a large grazing lease in the San Juans. When the time came for the friend to retire, the lease was sold to a rancher from near Monticello, Utah. The first time the new rancher moved his cattle up into the San Juans for summer pasture Chet followed, discreetly, at a distance, to make sure everything was going well. What he discovered angered him. Stray cattle appeared everywhere along the trail. Chet chased them out of the brush and up into the high basins where they belonged, but he couldn't help wondering why this man was so inept. At the end of a long day of picking up another man's pieces, Chet rode out, sad that this wonderful lease had gone to a man so ill-prepared to appreciate it. When he got down to the cabin that sat low in the valley near the trail head, he found that the man had left his cattle in the high country and returned to the cabin to sleep. But he had done so without unsaddling his horse or even bothering to remove his bit. The hard-worked horse was tied to the corral—still sweating, unfed, unwatered, and uncared for. Chet was outraged.

He walked into the cabin, grabbed the man, punched him up a bit, and delivered a lecture about what a good-for-nothing louse he was, then went to the corral, took care of the horse, and rode down the trail to his tent that was pitched up on a ledge near Lime Creek.

At about two in the morning, Chet was awakened by the sound of the San Juan County sheriff and the handful of sworn deputies who surrounded his tent. The sheriff called him by name and insisted that he come out of his tent with his hands up. The lazy bum who had so mishandled his cattle and abused his horse had taken exception to Chet's treatment of him, ridden into Silverton, and filed an assault complaint. Chet was taken into custody.

I saw him in Durango when he was out on bail waiting to go to trial. He told me the story and I asked him who his lawyer was. He answered, "Hell, I don't need no lawyer. I done the right thing. Any judge'll see that."

The judge didn't—and Chet did time.

Chet has done a fair amount of time over the years, but I don't think that bothers him too much. Jail time has almost always been served over matters of honor. And Chet is, above all, a man of honor. It's a part of his upbringing. Part of his idea of justice. Right is right and it's not always exactly the same thing as the law.

As much a part of the western heritage as the idea of honor and the proper treatment of working animals is the rich mythology of the Spanish gold mines. Every gold-mining region has its lore and nearly every region has at least one famous lost mine. In the San Juans, the lost mine is widely believed to be in the Twilights, the mountains that rise up from the Lime Creek Valley midway between Durango and Silverton.

The conquest of the New World was undertaken for many reasons. Certainly it was partly the urge to explore. Partly, there was evangelical fervor that carried priests into heathen lands seeking to save souls. More than anything, however, conquest fed greed and no one was more successful in feeding that greed than the early Spanish explorers who took gold back to Spain from the New World.

Stories of Spanish mines in the San Juans abound. Time has increased the mines' richness, and hidden their portals (if they ever existed). A few men, like Chet, spend their summers looking for gold, doing the things that all prospectors do, while they hold in the back of their minds the thought that a careful search, a lucky break, might uncover more than just a vein that has been overlooked—it might reveal the portal of one of the wonders of the world, a mine already tunneled into the richest of veins, a mine so full of gold that a man might carry enough out in his hat to live well for the rest of his years, a lode so full of gold that it had drawn men from across the ocean to mine it. This too is part of the heritage of the West and it was as real to Chet as the mountains that rose before him.

About ten years ago Chet and I went on a fishing trip. He asked me to bring along some climbing gear. I thought he finally wanted to learn how to use ropes and chocks so that together we might climb safely, for fun, when the fishing got slow. Usually we'd scramble up peaks; more than once I'd suggested that if he'd let me, I'd show him how to establish a belay, place anchors, and handle the climbing rope so that we could go to places we could only look at without them. He was never very receptive to the idea, but on this trip he surprised me by suggesting that I bring a rope and some hardware.

At the trailhead we unloaded his horse trailer, rigged the pack horses, climbed aboard our mounts, and rode off on a trail toward Elk Creek and the woods. We rode for a few hours, then rested the animals, picked up a few trout for dinner from the stream, then remounted and rode up into the tundra. It was when we arrived in the basin where we were planning to camp that I realized I had been brought along for a purpose, and it wasn't to tie flies.

We made camp well above timberline, pitching the large canvas tent in a flat open meadow. We rode the horses back down to timberline and filled the unloaded paniers of the packhorses with wood. After camp was properly made, the water bottles filled, and a pile of wood split and stacked by the tent, after the horses were cared for and set free to graze, Blackie hobbled and the roan given a bell around her neck, Chet turned to me and said, "How'd you like to do a little climbing?"

He pointed to a dark area on a high wall that he insisted was no more than fifty feet up from where a gully at the bottom of the wall ended and vertical rock began.

"I've always wanted a sample from up there," he said. "I think it might be a small portal."

We hiked to the wall, I rigged an anchor, and showed Chet how to belay me. I began to climb. Every fifteen feet or so I placed a chock, a runner, and a carabiner. I coached Chet about feeding rope. It was clearly more than fifty feet, more like a hundred fifty, and my short, hundred-twenty-foot rope ran out before I got to the top. I carried it behind me, unbelayed, and prayed that if I were to fall the friction of the long rope running through the protection I had placed would slow me enough to allow me to grab the rope myself, or a runner, or a flake with my fingernails—this was not the sort of thing I had hoped to be teaching someone new to climbing but he wasn't interested in climbing anyway. He wanted a sample. When I got to the ledge that sat before the dark place, I found an indentation in the wall, a kind of false portal. It was just deep enough to cast a dark shadow and it still looks like a portal to me from the valley below, even though I now know better.

I gathered rocks, broke off samples with a rock hammer, though I knew it was pointless, stashed the samples in my pack, and rappelled back down. About fifteen feet up from the place where I began climbing, I had to find some holds and leave the security of the rope. The rope hangs there to this day, I imagine, unless the marmots have been able to get to it or the sun has rotted it. I haven't been back to check.

When we got back to town we took a great many samples to Root & Norton for assaying. Bill Jones, the proprietor, issued his reports a few days later. Some of the rocks showed promise, but not the samples from the dark spot in the wall. That rock, he said, was "Leaverite." Leaverite? "Yeah. Next time you see rock like this, leave 'er right where you found 'er, it aint worth shit."

As discouraging as the assay report was, it really didn't matter all that much. I'm not sure that finding gold is so terribly important. It's the looking that matters. A person can do worse than spend the summers tramping about the mountains with horses, fishing for trout, scrambling the peaks, whether or not you ever find gold. Sometimes you fill your hat with something other than what you were looking for and that something other is even better.

I haven't seen much of Chet in the past few years. I've been working in the city a lot and my time in the mountains doesn't leave as much flexibility as it used to.

He called pretty often at first.

"Hey, Steve, you want to go up into The Twilights, do some fishing and look for gold?"

Well, either I couldn't because I was working or I had a house that needed tending or a family I wasn't getting enough time with as it was or I figured if I had a few days to spend any way I wanted to, I'd rather spend them fishing in the valley than hanging from walls with a rock hammer, gathering Leaverite.

But I heard stories about Chet every now and then, and every once in a long while he'd drop by the house and we'd chew the fat. After not seeing him for over a year, a mutual friend told me he'd heard that Chet had found a lost Spanish mine somewhere up in The Twilights and that he'd carried enough gold out in one day to pay all his bills and buy a new pickup truck. A few months later Chet stopped by for a cup of coffee and I asked him about it.

"Where the hell did you hear that?" he asked with a twinkle in his eye. His old pickup was parked in my yard, but he was sporting a nice new Resistol. "Naw, I aint found her yet." He grinned. "But how'd you like to do some packin' out of The Twilights next summer?"

I allowed as how my summer was getting pretty full and I doubted that I'd be able to cut loose for the weeks he was talking about. Too bad. Another hat full of gold sounds pretty good to me about now.

WHO OWNS THE RIVER?

Most fishermen prefer to fish their home streams. We often dream about distant water, fabled places where trout grow larger than they do at home, where salmon jump in the shadow of royalty, where bonefish run at blistering speed. Sometimes we actually make a trip to these distant places. I think it's safe to say, however, that most fishing takes place close to home and that most of us have a river or stream that we cherish as home water. In the deepest sense, water becomes home water when we take it into ourselves, when it becomes a part of us as real and inseparable from us as our arms and legs. To the extent that a stream has become a part of us, we own it. We own it like we own our thoughts and feelings. There is another meaning to the phrase, "we own it"; it comes from the concept of property. Is it possible, in this sense, to own a river?

It takes little wisdom, introspection, or knowledge of history to realize that many groups have had tenure on the land that surrounds our rivers. For most of the time that water has flowed on this continent past human inhabitants it has flowed past the people we call—continuing the error of Columbus—Indians. If claims made based on length of tenure have any validity, then all of our rivers and streams belong to the natives, but this is not the way of European law, and European law now rules the land. In the West we sometimes reduce the conflict of ownership to the simple metaphor of cowboys and Indians.

Cowboys and Indians have been struggling to make a go of it in the West for a long time and you would think that, having so much in common, the animosity between them would have simmered down. In some ways it has, but old ideas and years of mistrust die hard. The working cowboy never stole land from the Indian but he often took orders from those who did. The working cowboy knows and loves the land, and he is quite unlike the captains of industry who pushed towns and railroads westward. Although he rarely had much to do with the hard-driven, short-sighted, dollar-hungry industrialists and big-businessmen who managed the land of the West for short-term gain, the hard-working, land-loving cowboy is usually a white man, and to the Indian this spells trouble.

Real cowboys—people who live with, work, and move cattle, who earn their livelihoods on horseback—still exist in the West. They spend their days on ranches, sometimes staying with an outfit for life, retiring to less difficult chores and a modest cabin on a small piece of a large spread where they have spent the better part of their working years. Others move from ranch to ranch (and bar to bar) as the desire to move on overtakes their occasional need for cash. But real cowboys are a very small part of the working population. More do chores seated in the cabs and standing on the beds of pickups than riding on hard-leather saddles. Today, damn near everyone who wears pointy toed boots and a broad-brimmed hat and works outside thinks of himself as a cowboy. It's possible the true natives see it the same way.

Some whites who have spent a lot of time on the land, feeling both gentle breezes and harsh storm winds against their cheeks, the sun sometimes warm, sometimes brutally hot on their exposed faces, who have been close enough to the land to learn that its cycles hold knowledge more useful than the collected wisdom of textbooks, move in their thinking and understanding toward the traditions and ways of America's land-based and place-rooted natives. Many Indians find the allure of white towns and the abandonment of old ways to be a more attractive alternative than the almost certain material poverty that affirmation of the old ways brings. There are cowboys who are tinged with red and Indians who begin to pale. For the most part, however, we are each deeply connected, for good or ill, with our individual histories and traditions. The differences between us are real and profound.

A good friend of mine is a cowboy in the less restrictive modern sense. He rarely works cattle any more, though he was raised on a cattle ranch. Sometimes he helps out on a nearby sheep outfit—not, I suspect, because he needs the work, but because he loves the country that the outfit leases for summer pasture: the Cascade basin, a rugged place of spruce, fir, willow, and tundra surrounded by the jagged peaks of the southern San Juans. He loves to be outside, doesn't own a house, frequently stays with friends, but more often finds himself out in the woods somewhere working as a surveyor, riding about on the pretext of prospecting for gold, working sheep, hunting, or just sleeping out in a tent with his horses nearby because that's where he likes to be. Given his love of the land, his intimate knowledge of the terrain, weather, and wildlife of his home, I would have suspected that he would feel a strong kinship with those who roamed these hills before him, but this is not the case. At least not in actual fact. He embraces the romantic notion of the Indian of the past, the noble savage and all that, but show him a very real, very modern Native American and his position changes. Technically he's not a cowboy, but in the world of cowboys and Indians, there's no question where he stands.

Once, with a startlingly straight face he looked me in the eye and said, "I wouldn't give you a nickel for one of them Utes. Worthless. They can have a piece of land for years, and they'd never do a damn thing with it—never clear it for pasture—just let it sit and do nothin'. Now them Pueblo Indians, they're okay. They're just like us."

His reading of the history and ways of these people is appalling, but the ideas he expresses are all too common. Many of the Utes, having accepted the limitations imposed on them by the overwhelming horde of newcomers, have adapted and changed. Many farm and ranch, but that's hardly the point. A person with a long-standing and relatively recent tradition of hunting and gathering is quite unlike the European who settled into feudal, agricultural structures centuries ago. More to the point, that this cowboy expresses no guilt about herding sheep on land that was stolen from the Utes, land they had once freely roamed, makes any moral judgment by the cowboy suspect. We steal land and are good? An Indian decides not to clear pasture and is evil? And if he thinks pueblo dwellers are "just like us" because they now live, for the most part, in houses recognizable to Europeans, he's dead wrong. The animosity that exists between cowboys and Indians is not just seen in the movies. It's all too real. And it goes both ways.

The coal fields of the four corners region sit mostly on Indian land and are a major source of revenue for white men and red men alike. Cowboys and Indians often work together in the pits, but their lives separate abruptly when the working day is done. One year my birthday arrived when I was working with a survey crew, mapping an area of tribal land near the coal fields north of Kirtland, New Mexico. I'd planned an evening celebration with two friends from the crew in the nearby town of Farmington. When the work day ended, we bounced into town and headed for the first bar we could find. Too distracted to realize what we were doing, we burst through the door and, laughing a bit too loudly, we plopped ourselves down at the counter to order the first of many beers. It wasn't until we started to drink from the long-necked bottles that we realized we were in an all-Indian bar. A very large, very dark-skinned man with a long braid came over and asked if we'd like to hear a joke, but humor didn't seem to be the intention. Everyone in the place had stopped talking. I began to wonder if we were going to get out of this bar with all of our body parts attached to the same places they were when we walked in. Danny, who spent too much time dressed in green in Southeast Asia not to have a good nose for danger, looked a little worried. Kelly, who spent World War II in the belly turret of a B-17, looked like he'd just lost his landing gear. I don't know how I looked, but I don't think it was exactly jovial.

"Old Joe, an ignorant old Indian, was arrested by a white sheriff one night," the man began. "Seems the old bastard had been running around town making a lot of noise, and generally disturbing the peace. He was drinking too much and acting crazy. Hootin' and hollerin' he dropped his jeans and took a dump in the middle of the street. After pulling up his pants he stepped back and blasted away at the crap with his shotgun. Terrified, the white folks ran for cover. A stray cat wandered into view and crazy Old Joe blew him apart with another blast from the shotgun. Slowly Joe walked over, picked up the cat, and to everyone's horror he began to rip it apart and eat it. Finally, old Joe sat down on a curb by the side of the road. He pulled a bottle of whiskey, half empty, from his baggy pants. Raising the bottle to his mouth, leaning back with a bad wobble and almost falling over, he finished it off. With great anger he threw the empty bottle away, screamed some stuff, and fell asleep in the gutter. This is when the sheriff came out from behind cover and dragged the crazy, dumb, old Indian off to jail.

"'You crazy old Indian,' the sheriff asked the next morning when Joe finally woke up, 'why the hell did you raise such a ruckus last night?'

"'Hell, sheriff, I was just tryin' to be a white man like you. I was out there havin' a good time. You guys seem to like it so much, I thought I'd try it.'

"'What the hell do you mean?' the sheriff said.

"To which old Joe replied, 'yeah sheriff, the way I see it, that's all you white guys ever do—drink whisky, shoot the shit and eat pussy!'"

The man telling the joke wasn't smiling and the bar was dead silent. Danny, Kelly, and I looked at him, looked at each other, then damn near fell off our bar stools laughing. Slowly others began to laugh, and finally the whole place was in an uproar. The man who told the joke sat down next to me, nicknamed me "long nose," and helped give me a proper birthday celebration. It took a while for us to get properly drunk, but by the time we did there was a lot of back-slapping and joke-telling, name-calling, lying, and nonsense. It might easily have gone another way in this world of cowboys and Indians.

My home stream is a little one and I love her dearly. I travel and fish fabled water occasionally but I am always happy to return home, to see a canyon I know and to find cutthroat where

I expect them. It lies on breathtakingly beautiful land that was purchased from the Utes with broken promises. The significance of this fact is not lost on me. I know that the theft was an illusion that will not last, however. The white man who thinks he owns this stream is mistaken, and the native's grievous loss, a deep unhealing wound, is soothed with the sweet balm of truth. If you cannot own it you cannot steal it. You can no more steal a river than you can steal love.

LOST SOULS

The Animas River has flowed near my home for sixteen years now. I came under the river's influence when I moved to Silverton, not far downstream from its headwaters. I now live about fifty miles farther from its source. In all that time, through the change of address and the changes of seasons, the falling out of too much hair and the coming of far too many gray ones, the birth and growth of a child, the death of love, and then a loved one—and a good many of the other things that punctuate a life—the Animas has been there, outside the house, sitting quietly under the ice, roaring through the spring runoff or gently flowing through summer and fall toward another frozen winter.

Named by Spanish explorers who came into the San Juan country from the south, its source in the San Juan Mountains must have seemed distant, unapproachable, foreboding. How else can you explain a name as full of gloom as Rio de las Animas Perdidas— River of the Lost Souls. But it held no horror for the native people who hunted its valleys and followed game into the mountains that rise above its headwaters. Today the Animas retains its Spanish name (in abbreviated form, fortunately) and we can only guess at the impression it creates on those who see it. Few, I hope, continue to see it as a river of lost souls.

Though not a good trout river in its upper reaches, the Animas improves in this regard as it flows southward, down from the San Juans into the narrow valley that holds the town of Durango. The toxic flows (partly natural, partly the result of poisons flowing from abandoned and working mines) that degrade much of the water in the vicinity of Silverton have bubbled and bounced their way through many miles of canyons and gorges before they emerge in the valley above Durango. There the Animas flows in broad meanders that are reasonably pure and hospitable to trout. Past my front door (a block of homes and a band of riverside park distant) trout rise in a broad flat on summer evenings. Stocked rainbow trout are eagerly sought by local fishermen armed with everything from flies to Velveeta. Brown trout hold in the depths, usually waiting until dark to feed, and though sought just as eagerly, rarely end up on the stringers seen on this part of the river.

Just south of town the water begins to flow through a progression of broad flats, narrow shoots, and braided rock gardens, as gentle bottom land full of ranches and farms alternates with steep sandstone cliffs along the course of the river. This pattern— broad valleys alternating with steeply walled canyons—continues as the river flows toward its confluence with the San Juan River near Farmington, New Mexico, another fifty or so miles to the south. A lot of this is trout water. Some of it is good trout water.

A little of it is trout water so good, you wouldn't believe me if I told you just how good it is.

This morning I walked into a local second-hand bookstore where I picked up a clean used copy of Dana Lamb's *Where the Pools Are Bright and Deep*. I enjoy a good fishing story, especially if the story has a bit of myth to it (not the myth of complete fabrication, mind you, but the myth of allowing a fish, or a river, or even the occasionally monumental angler to achieve poetic, even epic proportions). The proprietor of the store is an ardent angler. As I was paying for the book, George struck up a conversation.

"Been out fishin' much lately, Steve?"

"Naw, George, mostly I've been working. But I have managed a few days on the Dolores in the past week; and one afternoon a few days ago I got a couple hours in on the Animas."

"Any luck?"

I looked around to make sure there weren't fifty tourists listening, ready to grab their rods and go kill fish as soon as they were told where to find them; seeing that we were alone, I told him, "Not bad really. I took a few small fish, but did nail one beautiful, wild brown trout."

"How big?"

"He went about twenty inches, maybe more, I didn't want to handle him too much so I just sort of stared at him to get an idea of his size before releasing him. I never got around to measuring him."

George now looked over his shoulder, down the aisles of bookcases stuffed with books, and turning back to me whispered, "I took a twenty-seven-incher from the river last week myself."

He told me the spot where he'd hooked his monster and it turned out it wasn't a hundred yards from where I'd hooked mine. This is one of those places we both know to be damn good trout water.

A few years back I wrote a book about fishing. It was a pretty thing, with lots of lavishly reproduced color photographs—the kind of book often referred to disparagingly as a "coffee-table book," and that's probably what it was. But I tried to write honestly and well; and, more to the point, I tried to be factual and accurate. The book had an illustrated appendix that consisted of a watercolor catalog of trout and salmon species and related game-fish, and was annotated with, among other things, Latin taxonomy. In the several years it took from writing to delivery, the genus of all the trout once called Salmo (other than Salmo salar, and Salmo trutta) had been changed to Oncorhynchus. So much for accuracy.

For this very reason, it may be foolish to write about fishing regulations in a book. Books seem to take longer and longer to come out, and anything said about something as changeable as fishing regulations will probably be outdated before a manuscript turns into a printed page. But there are reasons for writing about such things. While the laws that govern fishing on our rivers will likely change, the idea behind fishing regulations ought never change—that is, the need and desire to restore, preserve, and protect riparian habitat and rivers, the quality and diversity of life that dwells there, and as a result (and possibly as a matter of secondary value) to preserve the quality of fishing we enjoy and our children will enjoy after we have gone. I seriously doubt that the dominant conflicts affecting fishing regulations will ever change. Some people will always argue that it is an unacceptable economic burden to keep our water pure. Some will always claim that there are better uses for water than filling streambeds. And as long as there are fish to be caught, there will be those who want to catch and kill without limit. Some will simply want to provide food for their tables, others to generate income, and there will always be those who are trying to prove themselves in some way.

There will always be people who fail to grasp the simple fact that we cannot kill without constraint and still have fisheries worth fishing.

Although the Animas is, in some places, a splendid fishery, it is one that is at this time without protection. Because of the large population of good sized brown trout that live in some of its better runs, local conservation organizations (most notably Trout Unlimited) have begun a discussion with the state about getting some protection for the water.

The Division of Wildlife opposes any special regulations on the Animas. They present their argument in three parts. The first part of the argument has to do with the quality of the water. The second with the fact that only brown trout seem to have established a significant wild population, and since the average angler can't catch them they need no protection. The third and final part of the argument states that protection of a fishery through the imposition of special regulations alienates the vast majority of fishermen and ought to be undertaken very carefully. This last factor, it seems to me, influences wildlife management professionals more profoundly than any other. It sometimes appears to influence them more than their own studies of water quality and biological appropriateness. It certainly influences them more significantly than the arguments of conservation-minded anglers who often have a great deal of knowledge about the rivers for which they ask protection.

The state's position on the Animas River (presented to interested parties at a public meeting) included a lot of talk about the drainage as a whole. There was a map that showed the Animas and its tributaries in the vicinity of Silverton. All of this area was colored red and was described as a stretch of river through which dissolved toxins were added to the water at an alarming rate. In this area, we were told, fishing was poor to nonexistent because of the high levels of dissolved poisons in the water. A middle zone, extending through the southern reaches of the mountains and into the northern valley, was colored brown and described as an area in which the river, through the influence of uncontaminated tributaries and other factors, began the process of detoxification. The fishing here, we were told, was still quite poor. The area from Durango south was colored blue, and described as water in which trout could survive and some wild populations could be established, but not one which came up to the water-quality standards that would justify protection as "quality water." Brown trout had managed, we were told, to sustain themselves here, but no other stocked species had demonstrated much ability to do so.

The proceedings that evening reminded me very much of a similar evening I had spent with some weather consultants a few years earlier. Ski areas and the Bureau of Reclamation have a mutual interest in snowfall. The ski areas like it because when there's a lot of snow—early, late, and deep—they make a lot of money. The Bureau of Reclamation likes it because it fills their reservoirs with water and helps to sustain the greening of the West, a process not achieved without great cost, a lot of concrete, and the damning, rather *damming*, of a great many rivers. When reservoirs don't fill people ask a lot of embarrassing questions, like, "Can you assure us that all of this irrigation can go on indefinitely?" And, "Isn't it true that if nature calls this a desert, it might not always be a good idea to rename it farmland?" But I digress.

The weather consultants had proposed, with the enthusiastic support of the ski areas and BuRec, that "Snow Pack Augmentation" might be just the ticket. Cloud-seeding experiments were designed and several winters of making it snow earlier, later, and harder than ever before were planned. Needless to say, Silvertonians who had been shoveling the stuff from October to May, driving over the passes in blizzards, and those who had lost a friend or relative in an avalanche were not quite so enthusiastic. A town meeting was set up and a slick guy in a nice suit was sent to Silverton to tell us why we didn't have to worry about snow.

He, too, had a map. He, too, had some pretty solid scientific research to back up his story that we really had nothing to fear. He pulled out a study on orographic precipitation. He talked about the statistical averages for wind directions, storms, and precipitation levels. He said (boiling it all down to basics) that because Silverton sits where it does, and the storms come from where they do, the added snowfall from cloud-seeding would not come into Silverton. The mountains, you see, would catch the snow before the valleys.

Most of us sat there quietly, pleased that this nice educated man had taken the time to come and explain things to us. Most of us, but not all of us. From the back of the meeting room came a quiet, raspy voice. It was the voice of an old man who had lived in Silverton all his life. He wore a flannel shirt, worn jeans, and a wrinkled face. Calmly, and with great respect, he spoke to the scientist, the expert, the man with the nice suit.

"The way I hear you, the snow comes out of the clouds when the mountains lift up the wet air, making it colder, right?"

"Yes," said the expert.

"And mountains surround the town, and lift the air from most every direction it comes, right?"

"Exactly," said the scientist.

"So the storms get emptied out before they get to the valley, which means we got nothin' to worry about because all this extra snow you're promising the ski areas and the water people won't fall here 'cause it'll fall somewhere else."

"Right!" said the smiling face above the silk tie.

"So can you tell me one thing?"

"What's that?"

"How come it snows so damn much in Silverton?"

Now I don't want to appear to support anti-scientific, reactionary sentiment. I'm not saying that we don't need good, solid biological research to help us in our labors on the trout's behalf. What I'm wondering is whether common sense might not have a place here as well. If a study tells you that a river is marginal and a day of fishing gets you into big, strong, healthy trout; if you constantly hear stories from other people as well, people whose word you trust, that there are a good number of twenty-plus-inch trout in a river, you've got to wonder if the research that told you the river was "marginal trout habitat" might not be flawed. I'm looking for a raspy, quiet but respectful voice with which to say, "I understand what you're saying about toxins and recovery and marginal habitat, but can you please tell me, where the hell are all these big fish coming from?"

I'll tell you one other thing. As the word gets out about these magnificent trout it won't take too much imagination to guess where most of them will end up: with freezer burn, on wall plaques, killed, shown, and thrown away like so much garbage.

By the time this sees print, the Animas may well have had its wonderful population of large resident browns removed by the growing number of anglers who have become proficient enough to catch them. The river may be drawn so low, for irrigation, or to fill the reservoirs (needed to continue the illusion that there is no difference between farming the water-rich East and farming the arid West) that it is no longer suitable for trout.

Or, we could protect the river and the life it supports. Small trout would continue to rise in the broad flats beyond my front door, large browns hold near the boulders that provide cover a few miles downstream. Sections of water would be open to catching and killing what will be, by the very nature of the process, small, stocked trout, while those sections of the river that harbor the larger fish could be protected. My son may have the opportunity to fish the river he has spent his whole life beside, knowing it to be healthy and full of life. He may be able to fish for truly large, truly wild, truly wary trout. Or he may see the river and its fish die, knowing that the fate of this river is, in many ways, the fate of us all.

I really don't know which way it will go. Whatever happens on this river, I know that there are hundreds like it that will likely share its future. If the water is squandered, if the trout are forsaken, the river will live up to its Spanish name, and those lost souls will not be those of the big brown trout—they'll be ours.

OLD TIMERS

When I was a kid I went to work in Newark at my Uncle David's coffee shop. By the time I got to the neighborhood it was in decay. Though not yet the desperate, drug-ridden, and brutal area it would become in the seventies and eighties, it was surely no longer the stately neighborhood of large single-family mansions that it had been until shortly after World War II. City neighborhoods have strange cycles that defy understanding, at least my understanding. Fashionable neighborhoods sometimes remain fashionable for decades—and the wealthy continue to make their homes in them. Other neighborhoods gradually decline, until once stately homes become apartment houses filled with small, poorly maintained flats, their owners living elsewhere, collecting the rent and doing little to maintain the property. I've seen neighbor-

hoods fall and rise again with rediscovery and subsequent gen-
trification. I've seen others fall and continue to fall.

The neighborhood where Towers Coffee Shop was located
housed mostly old people when I worked there. There was a
home for pregnant teenagers nearby and a Catholic boys high
school, both of which are gone now. Each would send customers
who came, as often as not, in groups. Booths would fill with
strangely swollen young girls who waddled, who giggled sometimes, but who mostly seemed terribly sad. The young men from
the Catholic academy were clean and shiny in white shirts and
school ties, full of bravado and loud talk. Across the street there
was a supermarket. The customers who came from the supermarket were clerks and management on break. They raced in,
gobbled down egg sandwiches on Kaiser rolls, and rushed back to
work, all in fifteen minutes. A few other working people came in
for meals. My uncle Saul, who is a physician, had his office in the
neighborhood, and he would bring his staff for lunch every day.
They too would be pre-occupied by their work, but they'd linger
for nearly an hour. Waiting patients called them away from the
mahogany and red vinyl booths, the round mirrors against the wall
that were etched with art deco designs, back to the waiting room,
the examination rooms and lab. They had an urgency and sense of
purpose even when they were away from work.

Mostly, however, the customers were old people with no
place else to go.

I began working at Towers around the age of six or seven. It
wasn't really a job and I didn't get paid in cash until much later,
but my extended family often ate there, we gathered there, and we
were expected to help out if there was a need. Even the children.
Many Sunday mornings I would go with my mother and father,
my brother, before the doors opened at eight to collate the Sunday
newspapers that were sold at the coffee shop newsstand.

Towers carried the New Jersey papers—*The Sunday Star Ledger* and the *Newark News*—as well as the complete selection of New York City papers—*The New York Times, The Herald Tribune, The Sunday News, The Post, The Sunday Mirror*—and a number of others. Each paper arrived on Sunday morning in many different bundles. The news sections came in one bundle. The funnies, color magazines, and feature sections came in another. And a third carried the various advertising sections. Some papers had as many as six or seven different sections that needed collating. The amount of work to be done on a Sunday morning, just to get the papers collated, was incredible. Some of that work fell to the little ones.

As we grew, we assumed greater and greater responsibility in the coffee shop. From collating papers, we would go to waiting tables. By the time we were in junior high school, we were soda jerks, mixing egg creams with skill and panache. We could mix a little milk with a little chocolate syrup and seltzer and create a creamy chocolate soda with a pure white head (an art, I am told, that is slowly dying). From the fountain we went to the grill as short-order cooks. Finally, in high school, before leaving for college, we would supervise the other employees, run the cash register, and manage the place for Uncle David in those few hours when he was home.

We called it "The Towers Education," and it has served many of my cousins well. It isn't that I learned to make a good egg cream, and it isn't the ability to scramble eggs on a grill that has stayed with me, or, I assume, the others who graduated. What we learned was vastly more important than collating, cooking and waiting table.

The range of people who came through the doors was incredible. There were a few wealthy customers. There were far more poor people. There was a great deal of ethnic and racial diversity. Customers exhibited, boldly in some cases, their sexual preferences which were also diverse. It was the first place I had seen men kissing men and women kissing women. Some customers were terribly afflicted with disfiguring or crippling diseases. Many were old. Some very old. All were there to eat or drink, and it was our duty to provide them a service, and to provide it with respect.

It was there that I learned, no matter which side of the counter you are on, you are human. Whether the counter that temporarily divides you from another is a soda fountain or an office desk; a degree or a pile of money; a disease, a disability— we all eventually find that we spend time on both sides of the counter. We were all, I learned at Towers, engaged in the same enterprise. I worked there long before I ever heard the phrase "the human condition," but at Towers the concept developed meaning and form long before I was exposed to it in academe.

Beside Uncle David, who was the family philosopher and who had an aphorism for every occasion ("Excuses," he would say, shaking his head as you were starting to explain why you had screwed something up, "don't bother with them. Your friends don't need them, and nobody else will believe them"), those who taught me the most were the old people. Unlike the working clientele who rushed in and rushed out, the pregnant girls who kept to themselves and talked little with others, the Catholic academy students who talked a lot but were too young at the time to convey a lot of wisdom, the old people lingered. And they told stories.

The old timers would sit at the counter, drinking coffee and reminiscing. They would argue with each other about the details of an event that had taken place fifty years ago. A lot of the old men who hung around during the quiet times between rushes, in the evening when those whose families were still alive or still cared went home, were Italian. Many of the stories were mob related. Some were about tough guys and great Italian boxers. I heard about guys who were planted in the Hackensack River for being stoolies. I heard about the way the neighborhood used to be, how rich it was, and about the people who made it that way.

Sometimes three or four old timers would mount the pivoting stools between the Coca Cola machine that looked like a red outboard motor clamped to the middle of the counter and the cash register at counter's end, near the door. They'd talk loud and long, their hands gesturing wildly, their eyes rising to the ceiling for emphasis, crooked, smelly, thin cigars clamped between their teeth in the sides of their mouths, pouring smoke into the air. They'd tell stories. Stories of a past when they were young and strong and full of themselves, and the world was better.

Silverton seemed like home for a lot of reasons, not the least of which was the fact that it had a lot of old timers and that a lot of them were Italian. The Antonelli, Andreatta, Bonavida, Dallavalla, Giacomelli, Tedeschi, and Zanoni families were an important part of the town's history, and they were wonderfully proud of their role in building both the mines and the town. They too loved to sit around and tell stories, to argue minor details of events that had occurred fifty or more years ago. They too told me about the days when they were young and full of themselves, when the world was a better place.

Some of them, though old, were still pretty tough. I was in the Legion one day when a strong young Silverton guy walked in. He was loud and he was looking for trouble. The owner was Herman Dalla (the name was shortened some time after the family moved into the mainstream). Herman had been a boxer when he was young, but now, in his late sixties, he ran a bar. The young guy was disturbing his customers, so Herman asked him to be quiet. "Make me, old man," the asshole shouted. Herman dropped him with one punch.

These tough men came to the mountains from the Tyrol.

They came as miners. They lived on the mountain, at the mines in boardinghouses, many of them for months at a time. They saved money to bring their families over from the old country. When the families arrived many of the miners moved down into town and started businesses—confectioneries, groceries, bars. A few of them became involved in the nefarious activities of the red-light district on Blair Street—gambling, booze, and prostitution.

One old timer told me of the speakeasies during prohibition. "We didn't have to worry much," he said. "It was a town where very few faces were unfamiliar. An unfamiliar face set off alarms. We rarely had any problems. Every night we'd post someone up on the pass by the highway (there was only one road into town) and if someone strange came by, he'd beat it back to the joints and blow the whistle. By the time any government men showed up, everything would look legal."

I dated a wonderful lady from one of the big old Italian families in town for a while—and I got an earful. Once, when a proper aunt was lecturing my friend for getting drunk one night, she roared back, "Don't give me that. This family was up to its neck in booze during prohibition." The aunt left her alone.

If you want to know history, get it from old timers.

When the time came to get serious about fly fishing, I was in Silverton, and I guess something of the respect for old people and their stories that I had learned as a child stayed with me. Fishing, too, has its old timers, and they can teach you much more than technique. There is a great deal of wisdom to be gathered from them. The more I talk with fishing guides, and good young anglers, the more I realize how important the influence of old timers has been. One name comes up so often it almost seems as if he taught every good guide in the West to tie flies: Bob Crumm. Joe Kressl, who now lives on the banks of the

San Juan River in northern New Mexico, fishes with incredible skill and concentration. I believe he ties the finest flies I have ever seen. His guiding is gracious and he has the rare ability to help a client catch fish without making himself too visible in the process. He is humble and generous in spite of his prodigious talents. Where did he learn to tie flies? Who gave him his passion for trout and for fishing the fly? Where did he learn humility? From Bob Crumm. A. J. DeRosa is something of a legend up in Wyoming and Montana. He's a young guide with a passion for wooden boats, difficult trout, and adventure. He casts with awesome power. He nymphs with a sensitivity for the strike that is uncanny. He teaches angling with skill and patience, leaving every client with a bag of tricks and a good time. Who was his mentor? Bob Crumm.

I had my mentors, too. But they weren't as well known as Bob Crumm. My father disappeared before fly fishing became a passion for me and I landed in the San Juans with a lot to learn. The men who taught me knew little of the modern technique, and less about the revolution in materials (both fly tying and rod making) that was in the process of changing the face of fly fishing forever. What they did know were the streams and the fish. Men like Jim Bell and Gerald Swanson, both of whom were significant political and cultural figures in Silverton, fished too. They fished the fly. Both of them were primarily wet-fly fishermen.

The wet fly has taken a bad rap recently, having been replaced under the water by specific nymph, larva, and pupa imitations, and on top of the water by the various emergers and dry flies. In the last century a kind of dry-fly mystique evolved that led many to believe that dry-fly fishing is more difficult, and therefore more sporting, than wet-fly fishing. In some quarters the notion persists, but watching a man like Jim Bell swim a Dark Cahill quickly dispelled such nonsense. His casting was precise.

His drifts were calculated. I firmly believe he could sense at all times exactly where his fly was swimming, how it was behaving, and what he needed to do with the line to make the fish take. Most anglers can learn to do these things with a fly they can see. But to do it with a submerged fly is something else. The wet fly is a connection with the past. It is the fly of choice of many of the old timers I fished with. Because of them, I will always love it and fish it.

Gerald Swanson was a member of the Dalla clan. He was the butcher at Swanson's Market and for years the mayor of Silverton. His mother was Mary Swanson, who was a Dallavalla before marrying. Her sister married an Antonelli. The cousins and uncles and aunts of the Dalla/Antonelli family reminded me a lot of my own extended family and the meat counter at Swanson's Market was not terribly unlike the counter at Towers Coffee Shop. I learned a lot of history there.

Gerald and I talked fishing incessantly at that counter. I showed him modern fly patterns and new graphite rods. He was amazed. His favorite fly was the Pink Lady. Try to buy one of those at the Modern Angler Shop in your neighborhood. And Gerald never owned a graphite rod.

Gerald grew up on cutthroat. They needed little coaxing to take a fly, but would tolerate no sloppiness. A splashy cast, clumsy wading, a shadow thrown where it should not have been, and they would disappear beneath tree roots and rocks. Both Jim and Gerald emphasized careful stalking and careful presentation. It is a lesson that has served me well.

Gerald and I would share secrets. I would tell him when the fish were biting in the beaver ponds and which ponds were hot. I told him my secret places and he told me a few of his. He didn't get to fish much when I knew him, because he worked too hard. But when he did, he did well, and he did well with a Pink Lady.

He loved to hike the Snowflake Trail down from Molas Pass to the Animas River. Along the way he'd swim his wet fly. As often as not he'd take fifty or more fish. Wild fish.

In Silverton it was always the old timers who came out when things got tough, to make things right. It was men like George Bingle, who repaired the fancy equipment that younger men bought to keep the water flowing or the TV translator translating. It was George who always argued for simple solutions to complex questions, but saved all of our asses when complex things broke. The fancy machines inevitably broke. In the cold. In the snow. He fixed them, and never once said I told you so. I never got to fish with George. He died last year. I fancy he must have been a wet-fly man himself.

Jim Bell is gone too and I miss him. Gerald, younger than Jim and George, might resent me calling him an old timer. His stories are too damn good for him to be called anything else.

I love to hear old timers telling stories, especially outdoor stories. I loved to sit at their feet when I was little or lean against the market wall when I got a little older. I realized, even when I was little, that few things could bond men as well as a hunting trip or a fishing expedition, a lifetime of trips together, trips made with friends who remain friends for years. That these men had spent years loving the same things and doing them together impressed me more than anything else. And this, when I think about it, is the part of the angling tradition that moves me most. Not the tackle. Not the theory. The fact of people spending time together in the woods.

I have been wondering, if someone were to ask me to write down my most memorable fishing experience, what would it be? The biggest fish? The most difficult fish? The trip to the most distant or exotic place? At the moment, it is none of these. Special moments with good friends come to mind more readily than any of these. All of the really good memories seem to be of times with good friends, often old friends.

The day Hollis Holland and I first fished Lime Creek would be on that list. I guess the day with the deepest roots, the day most connected with the past, would be the last time I fished with Jim Bell up on the High Divide at Annabelle Lake. His lungs were bad and he could barely breathe, but he could damn sure cast. A fall afternoon when I watched Tom Montgomery nymph fast water on the Bighorn, taking big fish after big fish from a distant run, his casting flawless and graceful, his sense of the take uncanny, a big cigar chewed to a pulp stuck in the corner of his mouth while the Montana hills glowed golden from the setting sun—that day too comes to mind. There are days of spooky trout taken on tiny flies from clear, shallow water with Bud Collins that stand out. There are recent stories that I suspect will become framed in nostalgia with the passage of time; and if the friendships continue to grow, and we continue to fish together, some day I imagine we'll be sitting on a bench in downtown Durango, old and gray, telling them.

One day Bud Collins, Mike Crowley, and I found ourselves with a day off from guiding and a rare chance to fish together at the height of the season. We went to the Dolores River. Not many years back the Dolores had been a wild, untamed river that roared out of the San Juans in spring, slowed somewhat in summer, and dried to a trickle in the fall as a result of irrigation in the Montezuma Valley. But this was a new Dolores, below McPhee Dam. It was no longer wild and unregulated—but then, how many rivers are these days? The Dolores below McPhee Dam had become a super fishery. A tailwater. And it held some of the most magnificent cutthroat trout that anyone has ever seen. Many cutthroat over twenty inches inhabited the pools and riffles of the fishery below the dam. Each of us had fished the river a lot, but the three of us had never fished it together.

We separated to fish in the morning. We got together to eat our sandwiches and compare notes sometime around noon, when the fishing slowed a bit. Later in the day, when we figured the fishing should be good again we went to fish one last pool together before having to return to town. The last pool of the day was just below a piece of water called Turkey Flats. There were few fish in the main current, but across the river, about forty feet away, in a small eddy that sat behind a boulder, several fish were rising. Bud fished a Foam Beetle. Mike fished a Deer Hair Beetle. I clung stubbornly to a Thorax Adams. There was no hatch in progress, and beetles were working well on opportunistic feeders, but the Thorax Adams has a hold on me that is hard to explain, and it seems to take a lot of fish between hatches— during hatches, too, for that matter. I left it on my leader.

We took turns casting. Bud went first. The current was swift before the eddy, but dead where the fish were rising. Bud's technique was to mend rapidly, with repeated small mends, holding his fly still in the calm water of the tiny eddy until a snout came up, and the fly disappeared. Bud coaxed a trout from the eddy and landed it away from the other rising fish. It was a beautiful cutthroat-rainbow hybrid of about seventeen inches. Mike went next. He threw his fly into the eddy and looped a huge mend upstream in the fast current. His fly remained motionless, too, and a fine rainbow rose to take it. Then it was my turn. I chose to mend in the air. This, too, worked to keep the fly still in the slow water where the trout were rising. A trout took the Adams, and I soon landed a third fish.

We continued to cast in turn. Each of us landed two or three fish. Though none of us spoke much, I imagine that we were all feeling pretty much the same thing. After a season of fishing and guiding, each of us was unusually sharp. We were fishing well. We were fishing together. We were three friends on a river that each of us loved dearly—and we were casting to trout that we practically knew by name. There was a wonderful joy in the moment that bound angling with friendship, and with that very special river. When there were no more trout rising in the eddy, we looked at one another, smiled, and quietly walked back to the car.

Some day, if we don't drown, or have heart attacks first, if no one gets shot by a drunk hunter, if we escape disease and disaster, if we are lucky enough to spend long full lives fishing together in the mountains we love, we too will become old timers. We'll tell our stories and young hot shots will marvel that you could actually take a trout from the Dolores River with an Adams in those days. Unless the Bureau of Reclamation gets serious about managing the fishery they might even marvel that there were once trout in the Dolores River.

"Yep," we'll say, "you can fish those damn polypropylene and Lycra imitations all you want, but nothin'll ever replace a genuine muskrat Adams in my book. Naw, those were the days. The world was a better place. Gosh, we had us a time."

MOVING DOWNRIVER

I've become something of a city boy again with the move downriver from Silverton to Durango. A town of twelve thousand might not seem like much of a city to some, but these things are relative. For a long time I defined a city as any town that had a traffic light. Silverton had none. I drove through countless red lights when I worked in the small towns of Texas, because I just didn't expect to see them. When I was home, in Colorado, I wouldn't see one until I drove fifty miles south to Durango, the city, for groceries. I can remember days when even Silverton, with a population that was then in the neighborhood of eight hundred, was too much of a city for me.

Silverton is a headwaters town and it shares the characteristics and moods of the waters that surround it. Full of exuberance and adventure, it attracts people who are likewise. Durango is hardly sedate, but the river that flows through it is a bit more mature, somewhat gentler and broader. So too, it seems to me, are its inhabitants; but this is probably projection. My move from the headwaters to the valley has taken some time and my experience of the San Juans, bracketed by the experience of living in these two very different places, is framed in time and transition.

The ridge that was the High Divide, up the canyon past Howardsville, was visible from my bedroom window in Silverton. There I could watch storm clouds gather. The northern storms that rarely made it over the Divide into town would sit on that ridge in the winter and dump snow, while we basked in the sun a few miles west and south. Southern storms would roar up the canyon from Durango and shroud the mountains in gray. I knew when the southern storms came, although I could not see through the clouds, that the sky was blue on the other side of the Divide.

The storms that raged in the high country were unlike any I have seen at lower elevation. The air was often still, but the snow fell thick and steady. Once, in a twenty-four-hour period, five feet of the stuff came down in town. There's no telling how much fell up high, except that it was a lot. Much of that was pulled by gravity to the valley floor, roaring down in avalanches before time could settle the unstable snow into a lasting snowpack. After the storms had finished with us, moving eastward around the southern Rockies and then rolling northward and eastward through the plains, the wind would come. It would blow from the northwest. The sky would be brilliant, the sun yellow against the deep blue, but there would be no warmth, not for a few days anyway. Instead, a cold wind would build and snow would fly off the summits in great plumes that filled the blue sky with brilliant white clouds of blowing snow. Although the storm clouds were gone, a great wind would continue to rage up high on the peaks, and we would watch the contradictory sky.

Storms raged inside too. The late night panic that awakens the worried and troubled everywhere was more intense at altitude. The mountains, Dolores said, reflect your feelings back to you, magnified. This is unscientific, I know, but I experienced it too often to doubt the truth of her observation.

As intense and brutal as the storms might have been, it was not an unpleasant place. For all the bitterness of the nighttime cold, and the length of the season, there were winter days of blue sky and strong sun that could not be equalled elsewhere. I remember many days of skiing in January, skiing up high near thirteen-thousand feet, days of wallowing in light and warmth, days of loving the sun so much that if someone in the group hadn't insisted we leave, I'd have stayed on a high ridge until dark and probably frozen to death.

Downriver, in Durango, storms are less intense. We watch them from inside our homes and imagine what must be happening up in the mountains. Although deep snow can fall here too, it rarely does. A foot of snow is a big storm; two feet, a record breaker. I've never seen anyone tunnel to the woodshed, deciding in frustration that it would be easier to bore through it than to clear the snow, as I have seen people do upriver.

In Silverton I heated with wood for ten years. For eight of those years I cut, split, and stacked the wood myself. In the ninth year I bought rounds from someone else, and just split and stacked it. In the tenth year I bought it split.

My first year in the mountains, new friends—Dick and Betsy Armstrong—taught me to cut wood. Together we would take our chainsaws (theirs old, mine new) into the beetle-killed standing deadwood of Coal Bank Hill and cut. Together we would fell huge spruce trees and the occasional fir. Together we would limb and section the downed timber. Together we would load the aging, beat-up yellow Dodge pickup that belonged to the avalanche research station Dick and Betsy ran. Together we would crawl down into town in a truck that had lost its springs to the weight of the wood, that rode with the body snug against the axles. Each bump that we survived was a major victory, every corner from which the truck emerged upright a miracle, and the entry into town was always an incredible relief. There we would argue about who got what, each person trying to give the other more than he would take for himself.

Tom Hart taught me to split wood. I remember how difficult it was at first and how much easier it became when I learned to let the sun start the natural cracking of the rounds, to put my wedge in the weak places, to see the grain. I remember the day Tom and his wife Deborah drove over with a pickup load of wood and dropped it in my yard, because they knew I'd never get enough for that first winter at the rate I was going.

Today, downriver, I turn up the thermostat and I'm warm. I'm grateful that it works but there are few people to whom I can attach that gratitude.

Upriver, I fished like a child, scrambling over rocks, falling in the creek. I was wide-eyed with anticipation; every fish was an event. I was ignorant, but it hardly mattered. I held the illusion that my favorite stream was mine alone. I managed to fish, when I wanted to, every day for months at a time. In the middle of the day I would leave work and hike down into Lime Creek from the dirt road. I would find my own spots in narrow gorges and from the water I would pull good-sized wild rainbows. Jewels. Surprises. I could fish an Elk-Hair Caddis dry and a Dark Cahill wet, and nothing else. I could fish them big—tens and twelves; I could fish them on heavy leaders—three and four X. And I knew no Latin.

Which is not to say that life downriver is bad. Just different. I hardly ever fish every day for a month anymore. These days the periods of endless fishing seem to occur more often on vacation than as a part of everyday life. Still, if the snow is poor, and the urge to ski weakens, there will be winter weeks when I will fish two or three times on the tailwaters of the San Juan. And in the summer, some weeks will find me guiding three or four days and fishing on my days off. I still fish the Elk-Hair Caddis and the Dark Cahill on mountain streams. I choose these patterns for the memories as much as anything else. My boxes now burgeon with dozens of styles and patterns, some tied specifically for insects that have changed from bugs into *Pteronarcys californica* in the process of moving downriver.

There is a lot more time to think when fishing the broad rivers of the valleys. In the mountains the water moves fast. Here it takes its time. The casting is gentler, not the hurried picking of pockets but the calculated placing of drifts. The fish feed with a slower rhythm determined by hatches and do not grab frantically as food passes by. The imitations are smaller. The leaders finer. Between fish, between rises, I am more likely to sit on the bank and remember things.

I recall a tiny child who once staggered about on little skis, his rubber boots strapped into makeshift bindings. I see him falling and laughing and looking at me as if I were some kind of god because I could actually get those stupid skis to turn. I remember him growing to the point where he skied as well as I and together we roared down the mountain, carving long sweeping turns on steep slopes. And I remember the day when he asked me to follow him through some devastatingly choppy bumps and I could not keep up. He waited for me and graciously pretended that I could still ski as well as he.

The image of the day Daniel tied his first fly comes to me.

He watched me with great concentration, then repeated my actions perfectly, without any prompting. His first fly was a Wooly Worm and it was extraordinarily well tied. It took fish and was followed by inventions that made me laugh. The gold, red, and black bushy things he made were ludicrous, or so I thought. The neon-green and pink flies that were made from glo-bug egg yarn and dyed marabou were painful to look at, but they too took fish. I remember the day last summer when we stood shoulder to shoulder as Daniel cast a #24 midge pupae of his own design to large rainbows in a slow, shallow back channel. I see again the long drag-free drift and a large trout's white mouth beneath the surface. I can see Daniel gently lifting his rod to set the tiny hook. I see him carefully but quickly bringing a beautiful twenty-inch trout to the net. And I remember his smile. I see it all again, as my mind replays the events of that day.

Thoughts come of days spent on high mountain streams with a gentle woman who never fished, and I recall the pleasure of sharing lunch and conversation with her before she walked off into the woods, and I stepped back into the creek.

Sometimes when I am alone on the river I chuckle as I ponder the events that have taken me downriver. Love has found me again and I am giddy with it. Debbie and I were married last summer on a hillside above the Florida River. Debbie, who questioned the sick frog lure and the cannonball cast. Debbie, who pulled me into the water again, laughing.

A wedding canopy, made from dead aspen branches that had fallen to the forest floor on Missionary Ridge and handcast paper tendrils, surrounded us on our wedding day. Wildflowers picked from the edges of hay fields covered the makeshift pulpit and were woven into Debbie's hair. Below us, in a still pool, trout dimpled the smooth surface of the river.

Friends came to drink Durango Pilsner, eat pot-luck, play

volleyball, throw horseshoes, and remember that few things in life are as good as old friendships.

A piper brought out his bagpipe, serenaded the bride, then wandered off into a meadow, the sound of the pipes echoing from the nearby hills. Fiddle and guitar sang for the barefooted women who lifted their skirts to clog and for the older couples who waltzed together as if it were fifty years ago and this was the day of their wedding.

The rush of water flowing downstream carries memories and the sound of rushing water triggers images of the past. The farther downstream we fish, it seems, the more likely the images are to come. Fishing downriver is as much memory as anticipation; as much validation as hope.

My bookshelves, downriver from the headwaters, are filled with books I read many years ago. The tops of the low bookcases are piled with things I have read recently or have picked up in past weeks and hope to read soon. In the corner of my office there is a pile of fly-rod tubes and an assortment of fishing vests hanging from a hook on the wall. My closet is full of flannel shirts and wool jackets. Some of them smell pretty strongly of smoke and pine tar.

Sometimes when Daniel is with me, we will share this house and go about our business independently. I've caught him rummaging through my books, sitting on the floor, lost in concentration. I've stumbled upon him trying on vests, opening rod tubes, assembling and flexing fly rods. The sight always moves me.

I've given him old wool shirts from my closet to wear in the woods, so he won't ruin new ones, to maintain continuity, to be sure that he will never have to leave this house in order to find his father, although he may have to leave it to find himself. I give him reels that have lost their paint in my hands, in our mountains. I give them in the hope that he will always feel at home here in the San Juans.

My father never turned up. I didn't find him in the mountains. I didn't find him in the woods. The shadows that I have glimpsed and held have gone beyond counting, but he was not present in any of them. If I came here to find a home, I have been successful. If I came here to find my father, I have failed. But I have found other things.

My father is nowhere to be found, but I am a father now. My bookshelves, closets, and walls carry my father's imprint. His imprint is upon me. People tell me they see it in my eyes. My imprint is upon the child that I see before me. It is in his eyes too.

I hope that fly rods, wool, and flannel will fill his closets, along with the smell of wood smoke and pine; that books will fill his bookcases and that some of them will be mine; that someday, downriver, there might be a grandchild. Someday, downriver.